TABLE OF CONTENTS

Introduction 1

Red Teaming Background 6

Core Concepts of Red Teaming 7
___Core Concept: Challenge the Organization's Thinking 8
___Core Concept: Alternative Analysis 11
___Core Concept: Alternative Perspectives 14

Case Study 1: Field Marshal Slim in Burma 15
___Challenging the Organization's Thinking: 17
___Alternative Analysis: 21
___Alternative Perspectives: 27

Case Study 2: T.E. Lawrence in WWI 31
___Challenging the Organization's Thinking: 33
___Alternative Analysis: 36
___Alternative Perspectives: 41

Case Study 3: Operation IRAQI FREEDOM 44
___Alternative Analysis: 47
___Alternative Perspectives: 54

Conclusion 61

APPENDIX 1: Decision making theory and red teaming 66
APPENDIX 2: Background of Field Marshal Slim Case Study 68
APPENDIX 3: Background of T.E. Lawrence Case Study 79

BIBLIOGRAPHY 83

Introduction

In 1998, the Oakland Athletics floundered at the bottom of the American League West division of Major League Baseball. If you asked any number of baseball critics the reason, you would likely get similar answers. Conventional wisdom said that the Athletics were a small market baseball team and did not have the financial resources to pay the caliber of players that would enable them to compete with teams like the New York Yankees. Oakland was on the bottom end of the financial standings, posting the lowest or the second lowest payroll in baseball.

Just one year later, they improved their record to well over .500 and climbed into second place in their division. At the end of the 2001 season, they won more regular season games than any other team in baseball, except the Seattle Mariners. The 2002 season turned out similarly, as they tied the Yankees for the most wins in baseball. The Athletics have since continued their winning tradition, without a significant change in their payroll. How did they manage to turn baseball upside down? This question inspired Michael Lewis's *Moneyball: The Art to Winning an Unfair Game*, which is the story of how Billy Beane took a poorly financed, losing team from the "cellar" of the American League West to competing for league championships.[1] According to Lewis, the answer was that Billy Beane and the Oakland Athletics organization reinvented baseball knowledge.[2] In essence, Billy Beane challenged the organization's thinking,

---

[1] Michael Lewis, *Moneyball: The Art of Winning an Unfair Game* (New York: W.W. Norton and Company, Inc. 2003), XIV.

[2] Ibid.. XIV. Lewis states, "At the bottom of the Oakland experiment was a willingness to rethink baseball: how it is managed, how it is played, who is best suited to play it, and why. Understanding that he would never have a Yankee-sized checkbook, the Oakland A's general manager, Billy Beane, had set about looking for inefficiencies in the game. Looking for, in essence, new baseball knowledge. In what amounted to a systematic scientific investigation of their sport, the Oakland front office had reexamined everything from the market price of foot speed to the inherent difference between the average major league player and the superior Triple-A one. That's how they found their bargains. Many of the players drafted or acquired by the Oakland A's had been the victims of an unthinking prejudice rooted in baseball's traditions. The research and development department in the Oakland front office liberated them from this prejudice, and allowed them to demonstrate their true worth..."

incorporated alternative analysis, and exploited alternative perspectives in his decision-making on drafting baseball talent.

The conventional wisdom was that underfinanced baseball teams could not compete with teams who spent six times as much on players. However, necessity forced Beane to look for ways to disprove this conventional wisdom. The "old" baseball knowledge was that big league baseball potential existed only in players with the right "tools," and by a subjective evaluation of the player's "look."[3] Beane realized that the conventional wisdom of how to evaluate a player's potential was too subjective and caused scouts to overlook all sorts of baseball talent. He tried to develop ways to exploit this oversight.

To do this, he harnessed ideas from people who were outside of baseball. As Lewis observed, "…his scouting department was the one part of his organization that most resembled the rest of baseball. From that it followed that it was the most in need of change."[4] To overhaul this area of the organization's thinking, he used ideas from several baseball outsiders. One of these outsiders was Paul DePodesta, a Harvard graduate who never played baseball, but participated in the Athletics scouting meetings.[5] DePodesta used statistical analysis from his computer to understand the value of amateur players. Most of the players his computer recommended were anything but players the "old" baseball scouts would pick. In essence, DePodesta's statistical methods challenged the conventional wisdom of the "old" scouts.

Additionally, when Sandy Alderson hired Beane as the assistant general manager in 1993, he gave him a pamphlet written by Eric Walker, which explained the Athletics management principles on scouting. Lewis states, "This new, outsider's view of baseball was all about

---

[3] Lewis, 3 and 38.

[4] Ibid., 17.

[5] Ibid., 18.

exposing the illusions created by the insiders on the field."[6] Walker's ideas about judging the value of talent objectively challenged the conventional wisdom of the "old" baseball scouts who judged potential subjectively.

Another outsider who influenced Beane was Bill James. James shaped many of Sandy Alderson, Eric Walker, and Billy Beane's ideas on the value of statistics. Regarding conventional wisdom and statistics, Lewis states, "The statistics were not merely inadequate; they lied. And the lies they told led the people who ran major league baseball teams to misjudge their players, and mismanage their games."[7] James concluded that the naked eye was inadequate to judge how good a player was. He stated in his self-published *Baseball Abstract*, "One absolutely cannot tell, by watching, the difference between a .300 hitter and a .275 hitter. The difference is one hit every two weeks."[8] Yet, watching was exactly how the "old" baseball scouts assessed baseball talent. James's *Baseball Abstract* was exactly the type of thinking Beane was looking for.[9]

These individuals challenged baseball's conventional wisdom by coming at the problem from a different perspective and by using alternative analysis. All of these individuals were baseball outsiders with a different set of skills. DePodesta was an economist with interests in psychology. Alderson was a former Marine Corps Officer and lawyer. Walker was an aerospace engineer. James was a statistician and writer. None of them had any of the preconceived notions of the "old" baseball scouts. By challenging the thinking through alternative perspectives and alternative analysis, they invented new baseball knowledge that enabled them to find and exploit talent the "old" baseball scouts overlooked. The result of this new baseball knowledge enabled

---

[6] Lewis, 62.

[7] Ibid., 67.

[8] Ibid., 68.

[9] Ibid., 69. Lewis notes, "It was James's first sustained attack on baseball's conventional wisdom."

the financially challenged Oakland Athletics to compete successfully with teams commanding several times the financial resources.

You might ask yourself, "What does all this have to do with military decision making?" The answer is that Billy Beane and the Oakland Athletics baseball experiment is a quintessential case study in red teaming. Red teaming improves decision-making. That means baseball decision-making or military decision-making. Just as Billy Beane freed himself from the "old" baseball knowledge by challenging the conventional wisdom, exploiting alternative perspectives and incorporating alternative analysis of his operational environment, military commanders can use the same tools to improve decision-making.

Numerous studies conclude that the Department of Defense needs the type of thinking behind the red teaming concept in order to meet the challenges of the twenty first Century. The Defense Science Board conducted a study in 2003, and concluded "...red teaming is especially important now...Aggressive red teams challenge emerging operational concepts in order to discover weaknesses before real adversaries do."[10] Additionally, the Institute for Defense Analysis concluded, "A strong red team is needed to expose weaknesses and foster robustness in proposed concepts..."[11]

The recent emphasis on red teaming throughout the DOD implies that red teaming is a new tool for decision-making. However, military theorists throughout history emphasized the core concepts of red teaming, so it is anything but new. Some of the ancient military axioms have red teaming flavors to them. Sun Tzu's famous axiom, "...one who knows the enemy and knows himself will not be endangered in a hundred engagements" advocates the necessity for developing

_____

[10] Gold,Ted and Bob Hermann. *The Role and Status of Department of Defense Red Teaming Activities* (Washington D.C.: Office of the Under Secretary of Defense for Acquisition, Technology, and Logistics, Defense Science Board Task Force, 2003), Cover Memorandum to the Chairman of the Defense Science Board.

[11] John Sandoz, *Red Teaming: A Means to Military Transformation* (Alexandria Virginia: Institute for Defense Analysis, Advanced Warfighting Program 2001), 2.

a complete understanding of the environment through the adversary's perspective.[12] Clausewitz' *On War* emphasizes the need for critical analysis and challenging conventional wisdom and assumptions.[13] These are only two examples in a plethora of literature on warfare showing military commanders and theorists emphasizing the core principles of red teaming.

As late as World War II, U.S. military commanders successfully employed the key concepts of red teaming. Somewhere along the way, however, we seemingly lost sight of these core concepts. Strategic and operational level planning for Korea, Vietnam, Somalia, and Operation Iraqi Freedom epitomize failures in understanding the operating environment. Only recently have the services attempted to reincorporate the core principles of red teaming into decision-making and doctrine. Although it is only a cursory discussion, the January 2005 edition of U.S. Army FM 5-0, *Army Planning and Orders Production*, introduces red team principles into the army problem solving method.[14] Additionally, TRADOC staffed and funded the University of Foreign Military and Cultural Studies at Fort Leavenworth, Kansas, which educates, trains, and provides practical experience to red teams in order to establish a force-wide red team capability.[15]

Studying how great commanders in history used the core principles of red teaming may help solidify the U.S. Army's red teaming doctrine. Therefore, this monograph will compare the success of past "great captains" of warfare against relatively modern military failures of the U.S. Army in order to determine the necessity of using the core concepts of red teaming in the current

---

[12] Sun Tsu, *The Art of War,* trans. Ralph Sawyer (New York; Westview Press 1994), 179.

[13] Carl Von Clausewitz, *On War*, ed. Michael Howard and Peter Paret (Princeton, New Jersey: Princeton University Press, 1976), 156. Clausewitz states "the influence of theoretical truths on practical life is always exerted more through critical analysis than through doctrine," and "...it is vital to analyze everything down to its basic elements, to incontrovertible truth. One must not stop half-way, as is so often done, as some arbitrary assumption or hypothesis."

[14] U.S. Department of the Army, *FM 5-0 Army Planning and Orders Production* (Washington D.C.: Government Printing Office, January 2005), 2-4 to 2-5.

[15] Gregory Fontenot, "Seeing Red: Building a Red Team Capability for the Blue Force," *Military Review* 85, no. 5 (2005): 7.

U.S. army and Joint decision-making processes. To this end, this monograph presents three case studies to analyze military campaigns that successfully used the core concepts of red teaming and campaigns that did not. Each case study evaluates the extent to which the campaign included the core concepts of red teaming, and their implication on success or failure. This monograph's thesis is that the red teaming core concepts can significantly improve understanding of the operational environment and lead to better decisions.

Red Teaming Background

How do some commanders achieve such resounding success and others do not? As it did in the *Moneyball* story, the concept of "red teaming" provides part of the answer. The term "red team" is a relatively new buzzword used in military and civilian enterprises. However, there is no common understanding between or within organizations of what red teaming means. Businesses, governmental agencies, the Department of Defense, and each of the services have their own definition of red teaming and views on how to apply it.[16] Red teaming can mean threat emulation, also known as "role-playing the adversary", which is how the U.S. Marine Corps uses the term.[17] Another common meaning is conducting a vulnerability assessment of a process or system design to determine its weaknesses.[18] Finally, red teaming can mean using analytical techniques in order to improve intelligence estimates and intelligence synchronization, common in the DOD and governmental intelligence agencies.[19]

---

[16] Gold and Hermann, 2.

[17] U.S. Department of the Navy. HQ, United States Marine Corps. *MCWP 5-1, Marine Corps Planning Process*. Washington D.C.: Government Printing Office, 24 September 2001, 2-6. The Marine Corps Planning Process describes the function of the red cell as assisting the commander in assessing courses of action against a thinking enemy. The Marine Corps red cell primary responsibility is to role play the enemy during the wargame.

[18] University of Foreign Military and Cultural Studies. *Red Team Handbook version 3 draft*. 19 January 2007. Fort Leavenworth, Kansas: U.S. Army Training and Doctrine Command, 9.

[19] Ibid., 9.

While these definitions seem unrelated, they have in common the ultimate goal of improving decision making through critical thinking and analysis. This commonality forms the basis of the U.S. Army understanding of red teaming. The U.S. Army defines red teaming as "a function executed by trained, educated, and practiced team members that provides commanders an independent capability to fully explore alternatives in plans, operations, concepts, organizations, and capabilities in the context of the operational environment and from the perspectives of our partners, adversaries, and others."[20] The key aspects of this definition are its emphasis on independent thinking, challenging the thinking inside the organization, incorporating alternative perspectives in an attempt to eliminate cultural and ethnocentric bias, and a focus on fully exploring alternatives.

As warfare continues to become more complex due to the advent and proliferation of new technology, blending of ethnic and cultural groups, urbanization and population growth, and tendency towards asymmetric warfare, the core concepts of red teaming are even more important in order to achieve success on the battlefield. Only through a complete understanding of the operating environment from the perspective of the U.S., its adversaries, and local inhabitants of the operational area combined with critical analysis in decision making and planning can the U.S. Army successfully accomplish the diverse and complex missions looming in the future.

Core Concepts of Red Teaming

Critical thinking forms the foundation of red teaming. In *The Miniature Guide to Critical Thinking Concepts and Tools*, Dr. Paul and Dr. Elder sum up the reasons our thinking and problem-solving ability sometimes goes afoul in their assertion that, "…much of our thinking, left to itself, is biased, distorted, partial, uninformed or down-right prejudiced."[21] Just as their guide

---

[20] Red Team Handbook, 13.

[21] Linda Elder and Paul, Richard. *The Miniature Guide to Critical Thinking Concepts and Tools. 2nd Ed.*. (Dillon Beach, CA: The Foundation for Critical Thinking, 2005), 1.

seeks to improve critical thinking skills of individuals, red teaming seeks to improve critical thinking of a decision-making organization. Whether individual or organizational critical thinking is improved, Dr. Paul and Dr. Elder assert that one result is "open-mindedness within alternative systems of thought, recognizing and assessing assumptions, implications and consequences."[22] These are all areas of decision making that red teaming seeks to improve.

Although the U.S. Army concept for implementing red teams revolves around establishing an independent capability to assist commanders in decision-making, nothing prevents commanders from using these core concepts in their decision-making process without an "assigned" red team. There is no question that independent red teams can make significant contributions to decision making. Even the most experienced and knowledgeable commanders and staffs are vulnerable to the common pitfalls of planning and decision-making. However, without the benefit of these independent red teams, the commander and staff can simply do the thinking behind these concepts themselves. Critical thinking and the application of the core concepts of red teaming is the key. The three core red teaming concepts are challenging the organization's thinking, alternative analysis, and alternative perspectives.

Core Concept: Challenge the Organization's Thinking

The first core concept of red teaming is challenging the organization's thinking. Often, the modes of thought inside an organization inhibit understanding the environment or situation. Red teaming counters bad organizational thinking by challenging assumptions, playing the "devil's advocate", and challenging the "conventional wisdom."

Often, decisions makers fill gaps in knowledge or understanding by making assumptions. By challenging these assumptions, decision makers can improve decision making within their organization. Assumptions are information accepted as truth in the absence of facts, and they

---

[22] Elder and Paul, 1.

come in the form of explicit and implicit assumptions.[23] Decision makers treat assumptions as facts as long as they meet the criteria that they are essential to continue planning and are likely to be true. Both types of assumptions contribute to a decision maker's model of reality. As Dörner notes, "…assumptions about the simple or complex links and the one-way or reciprocal influences between variables constitute what we call that individual's reality model.[24]

Implicit assumptions are more difficult to deal with and cause more problems for decision makers. Often, decision makers are unaware of their implicit assumptions. They are the result of mirror imaging, ethnocentrism, paradigm blindness, faith in trends, cultural contempt, and biases. These implicit assumptions skew the decision maker's understanding of the operational environment, the problem, and potential solutions. Challenging the conscious or unconscious thinking behind these assumptions first alerts the decision maker that they exist, and then enables him to assess how they skew his understanding. Incorporating alternative analysis to identify and challenge these implicit assumptions facilitates a better understanding of the operational environment and enables the decision maker to construct a more accurate mental model of the system.

Explicit assumptions are easier to deal with because planners identify them in the planning process. While the factors that generate implicit assumptions can also influence explicit assumptions, at least the decision maker is aware that they exist. This enables the decision maker to consciously analyze the impacts of the assumption on the decision making process and the assumption's validity. In fact, doctrine prescribes that decision makers continually seek to

---

[23] FM 5-0, 2-8.

[24] Dietrich Dörner, *The Logic of Failure: Why Things Go Wrong and What We Can Do To Make Them Right* (New York: Metropolitan Books, 1996), 41. Speaking of an individual's reality model, he also notes, "as a rule it will be both incomplete and wrong."

confirm or deny their assumptions.[25] Alternative analysis helps decision makers in this regard, as it expands the decision makers understanding of the system.

Another manifestation of challenging the organization's thinking is playing the "devil's advocate." The term "devil's advocate" originates from the Roman Catholic Church Canonization Process, in which the Sacred Congregation of Rites appoints an officer to challenge the character and argue against canonization of a particular candidate. Pope Sixtus V instituted the office in 1587, with the title "Promoter of the Faith" or "devil's advocate." The officer's duty required taking a skeptical view of the candidate's character and critically examining the other side's evidence in order to ensure only the truly worthy were canonized.[26] This process of taking a skeptical view ensured that only the best candidates achieved sainthood. Similarly, by employing a "devil's advocate," decision makers can expose weaknesses and ensure all aspects of the problem receive due care.

Finally, decision makers can challenge organizational thinking through challenging the conventional wisdom. Conventional wisdom comes from experience, which offers obvious advantages to decision making. However, it also brings some disadvantages. It sometimes results in what Dörner calls "Methodism,"[27] Dörner defines Methodism as "the unthinking application of a sequence of actions we have once learned," which can cause decision makers to "deconditionalize (sic) a form of action and use it over and over again if it has proved successful for us or for others."[28] Dörner asserts that Methodism stems from "automations," which are

---

[25] FM 5-0, 2-8.

[26] R.L. Burtsell, *The Catholic Encyclopedia Volume I*, trans. Cloistered Dominican Nuns of the Monastery of the Infant Jesus, Lufkin, Texas (New York: Robert Appleton Company, 1907)

[27] Dörner, 45. Dörner borrowed the term "methodism" from Chapter four, Book two of Clausewitz' *On War*.

[28] Ibid., 170.

sequences of actions that we carry out in everyday life, similar to reflexes.[29] While these "automations" provide many benefits, they can also limit our ability to see new possibilities. As Dörner notes, "experience can also make us dumb."[30]

Clausewitz' tree felling metaphor is instructive in describing the dangers of applying Methodism to complex situations. He states, "War consists of single, great, decisive actions, each of which needs to be handled individually…It is like a stand of mature trees in which the ax has to be used judiciously according to the characteristics and development of each individual trunk."[31] Challenging conventional wisdom enables decision makers to mitigate the effects of relying on methods simply because they worked in the past, and prevents applying cookie cutter solutions to unique problems.

Core Concept: Alternative Analysis

The second core concept of red teaming is incorporating alternative analysis in decision-making. Alternative analysis is the process of offering different understandings of the environment, the problem, potential solutions, and the vulnerabilities of the adversary and the decision maker.

An essential element of incorporating alternative analysis into decision-making is ensuring the decision maker has a complete understanding of the operational environment. Alternative analysis facilitates a more complete understanding of the operational environment because it enables the decision maker to construct alternative mental models of the system and its interrelationships from different perspectives and with different areas of expertise. This enables

---

[29] Dörner, 169.

[30] Ibid., 170.

[31] Clausewitz, 153.

the decision maker to synthesize the various perspectives and develop a better understanding of the operational environment.

Often, decision makers build their understanding of the operational environment from a single perspective, with incomplete or inaccurate information. Decision makers construct a mental model of the system based on this perspective, and although it may be flawed, this model becomes their understanding of reality. As Dörner states, "…we often do not realize that we are captives of our old ideas and are by no means considering all the available possibilities."[32] Additionally, Klein asserts that mental models carry emotional attachment, which encourages explaining away conflicting evidence.[33] However, the operational environment, or system, might function quite differently from the decision maker's mental model.

Alternative analysis also contributes to better decision making in the area of defining the problem. Obviously, a clearly defined problem sets the stage for success in problem solving. However, a common error in problem solving occurs in the first step: identifying the problem.[34] Often, decision makers misidentify the symptoms of the problem as the problem itself.[35] This is because the symptoms are generally the first observable signs that a problem exits, so the decision maker mistakes these symptoms as the problem. Misidentifying the symptoms of the problem as the problem itself causes decision makers to focus on solving the symptoms, leaving the root cause of the problem unsolved. In many cases, decision makers never truly understand what comprises the problem.

---

[32] Dörner, 159.

[33] Gary Klein, *Sources of Power: How People Make Decisions* (Cambridge, Massachusetts: The MIT Press, 1999), 68.

[34] FM 5-0, 2-6. FM 5-0 describes the U.S. Army problem solving method as a seven-step process: identify the problem, gather information, develop criteria, generate possible solutions, analyze possible solutions, compare possible solutions, make and implement the decision. It describes problem identification as recognizing and defining the problem.

[35] Ibid., 2-6.

Incorporating alternative analysis into decision-making can compensate for this difficulty to define problems because it offers different understandings of the problem boundaries. This alternative analysis focuses on "setting" the problem instead of solving the problem, a concept rooted in the emerging concept of systemic operational design.[36] "Problem setting" is essentially considering the overall problem context, and then defining the boundaries of the system. Bounding the system and focusing on those aspects of the system that impact the problem context is essential to accurate problem identification. By looking at the boundaries from a variety of perspectives, decision makers can accurately identify the causes of the problem.

Additionally, the operational environment is composed of complex adaptive systems, which significantly confound problem definition. John H. Holland describes complex adaptive systems as "a dynamic network of many agents acting in parallel, constantly acting and reacting to what the other agents are doing…the overall behavior of the system is the result of a huge number of decisions made every moment by many individual agents."[37] A common error in problem solving is that decision makers fail to account for this adaptive capability. As Dörner notes of the "bad participants" in his Tanaland experiment, "the participants apparently felt that their initial questioning and reflection gave them a sufficiently accurate picture of the situation, one requiring no further correctives, whether by gathering additional information or by reflecting analytically on the results achieved. They thought, mistakenly, that they already had the knowledge they needed…"[38] Conversely, he notes that for the "good" participants "the problems

---

[36] William Sorrells et al., "Systemic Operational Design: An Introduction" (School of Advanced Military Studies Monograph, Fort Leavenworth, Kansas:, U.S. Army Command and General Staff College, 2005), 15.

[37] John Holland, *Hidden Order: How Adaptation Builds Complexity* (Reading, Massachusetts: Addison-Wesley Publishing Co. 1995), 55.

[38] Dörner, 16-17. Dörner's Tanaland experiment is a computer-generated simulation designed to analyze decision-making effectiveness and strategies of individual participants in a complex environment. Each participant had the task to promote the well-being of Tanaland's inhabitants and the entire region. Each participant had dictatorial powers to carry out any measures they desired without opposition. During the experiment, the participants had six opportunities to gather information, plan measures, and implement

of the situation underwent redefinition."[39] The complex and adaptive nature of the operational environment requires continuous reassessment of the problem definition, or iterative learning. Using the concept of alternative analysis in problem definition enables decision makers to account for this complex and adaptive nature of problems.

Finally, alternative analysis assists decision makers in identifying friendly and adversary vulnerabilities. By taking a critical look at the friendly plan to identify potential areas where the plan could go wrong, oversights, flaws in reasoning, and potential long-term repercussions and side effects, alternative analysis can expose weaknesses in the plan before it is too late. As the Defense Science Board Task Force on the Role and Status of Red Teaming states, red teaming can "…discover weaknesses before real adversaries do."[40] One method of doing this is Klein's "pre-mortem strategy."[41] Similarly, alternative analysis takes a critical look at the adversary in order to identify areas susceptible to exploitation.

Core Concept: Alternative Perspectives

The third core concept of red teaming is incorporating alternative perspectives into decision-making. An alternative perspective is the view of the operational environment as seen through the cultural lens of the adversary, coalition partners, and other actors within the system. Often, decision makers fail to account for these perspectives and base their decisions solely on their own perspective. Mirror imaging, and ethnocentrism contribute to this inability to account for the perspective of others. By understanding these tendencies and accounting for these alternative perspectives, decision makers can better anticipate second and third orders effects, as well as anticipate the strategic and operational implications of their actions.

---

decisions over the course of ten years in the simulation. In each of the planning sessions, the results and impacts of previous decisions were available to the participants.

[39] Dörner, 17.

[40] Gold et al, Cover Memorandum to the Chairman of the Defense Science Board.

[41] Klein, 71. For more on Klein's "pre-mortem" strategy, see appendix 1.

Mirror Imaging occurs when decision makers apply their beliefs, cultural concepts, and values to others. These normative concepts guide the decision maker's actions. However, the beliefs, cultural concepts, and values of other actors can differ from the decision maker's, which causes these other actors to perceive the environment and act in completely different ways than the decision maker might expect. Thus, the decision maker must understand the perspective of the other actors to predict their actions and the effects of our actions on them.

Ethnocentrism is another factor that causes decision makers to overlook the perspective of other actors. Ethnocentrism is the inherent belief in the superiority of ones own culture or ethnic group. Unlike mirror imaging, ethnocentrism recognizes differences in beliefs, cultural concepts, and values, but discounts them as inferior or fails to understand them. This belief in the inferiority of other cultures and ethnic groups causes decision makers to underestimate or misunderstand the adversary or other actors. Incorporating alternative perspectives enables decision makers to understand the beliefs, cultural concepts, and values of other actors, thereby improving understanding of the situation or problem, and facilitating better solutions or courses of action.

Case Study 1: Field Marshal Slim in Burma

On March 19, 1942, Field Marshal Viscount Slim assumed command of the British Army Burma Corps, later renamed Fifteenth Corps, which was engaged in a struggle to hold Burma against a better trained, better equipped, but numerically inferior Japanese force.[42] At the time, Slim knew almost nothing of the enemy he would fight for the next three years. In his account of the Burma campaign, entitled *Defeat into Victory,* he remarks, "I reflected…how very ignorant I was of the Japanese, their methods and their commanders."[43] He was about to learn much more

---

[42] Michael Calvert, *Slim* (New York: Ballantine Books, Inc. 1973), 31.

[43] William Slim, *Defeat Into Victory: Battling Japan in Burma and India 1942-1945* (New York: Cooper Square Press: Distributed by National Book Network, 2000), 20.

about them. This case study examines how Slim turned a devastating defeat "he" suffered in the

1942 Burma campaign into resounding victory by the end of 1945. Over the next three years,

Field Marshal Slim endured crippling defeats during a long and costly retreat from Burma into

India, assumed command of the Fourteenth Army, retrained his Army in India, and then

counterattacked to retake Burma in a brilliant campaign that turned "defeat into victory" for the

British Army in Burma.[44] Field Marshal Slim's 1945 counteroffensive demonstrates the value of

challenging the organizations thinking, incorporating alternative analysis, and using alternative

perspectives to improve decision-making.

Between the initial Japanese attack into Burma on January 20 of 1942, and Field Marshal

Slim's arrival, the Japanese soundly beat back the Burma Army, handing them defeat after defeat.

Slim's arrival in Burma did nothing to slow the Japanese advance, and the Japanese pushed the

British entirely out of Burma. Slim led a defeated army on a long and dangerous retreat out of

Burma with the Japanese Fifteenth Army nipping at their heels and the torrential monsoons

confounding every move.[45]

However, Slim did not let the horrendous experience of the long retreat out of Burma go

to waste. He immediately set out to gain a better understanding of his new adversary, the reasons

for the devastating defeat, and the environment so that he could prepare his forces to retake

Burma from the Japanese.[46] Armed with this new understanding Slim counterattacked into

Burma with the purpose of not just retaking Burma from the Japanese, but destroying the

---

[44] Slim, 551.

[45] Ronald Lewin, *Slim: The Standardbearer* (London: Leo Cooper, Ltd.; Octopus Publishing Group, 1976), 79. Lewin notes, "Once the Japanese decided to move aggressively into Burma no commander, living or dead, could have sustained by his genius the indefensible British position. It was a house of cards, erected on the quicksands of false hope.

[46] A more detailed study of the background of this case study and Field Marshal Slim's analysis of the environment and his training program is located at Appendix 1.

Japanese Army in Burma.[47] The campaign took eight months, consisted of several key battles on which the fate of the campaign rested, and cost the Fourteenth Army many casualties. It cost the Japanese much more, however. Slim's Fourteenth Army mostly destroyed the Japanese forces in Burma, and by the end of March 1945, the Japanese commander realized he could not hold onto Burma and evacuated his remaining forces into Thailand.[48]

Given the dire circumstances under which Slim assumed command of the Fourteenth Army, the general condition of the Burma Army after the retreat, the miserable conditions caused by the terrain and weather, and the extremely low level of attention and priority given to the Burma Campaign, Slim's hard-fought victory in Burma was anything but predetermined. Although he would not have used these terms, Field Marshal Slim applied the core concepts of red teaming in his success. Using red team concepts, Slim's army overcame the seemingly insurmountable obstacles the Burma Campaign presented. He challenged his organization's thinking in the areas of the British capability to fight in the jungle, and in their over reliance on motor transportation and on supplies. He incorporated alternative analysis in their use of air assets for movement, re-supply, and in treatment of casualties. Finally, he incorporated Chinese and Japanese perspectives into his decision-making, which enabled him to anticipate Japanese strategies and plans.

Challenging the Organization's Thinking:

The most important way in which Field Marshal Slim challenged the organization's thinking was in the area of the British capability to fight and win in the jungle against the Japanese. Over the course of the 1942 campaign, the Japanese soundly defeated British forces because of the British inability to operate in the jungle, and the seeming ease and skill the Japanese forces showed in them. This resulted in a sense within the British forces that the jungle

---

[47] Slim, 184.

[48] Ibid., 486.

was a "strange, fearsome place; moving and fighting in it was a nightmare."[49] Slim observed that

to the British forces, the jungle was an obstacle impeding movement and vision. To the Japanese,

however, it was a means of concealed movement and surprise.[50]

Slim knew he had to dispel this fear of the jungle and the belief that the Japanese were

superior in it before his Fourteenth Army could beat them.[51] Based on this, his training regimen

in India focused on getting his men comfortable and proficient in jungle operations. His training

succeeded in building confidence in his men, but he had to dispel the myth of Japanese

invincibility as well. To capitalize on this basic confidence in jungle operations, he recognized

that he needed his men to fight and beat the Japanese in small-scale engagements and ultimately

large battles.[52] He started with small scale patrolling into the border area and minor offensive

operations against Japanese advance detachments in which Slim ensured his forces always held a

numerical advantage.[53] His units achieved success, which built a sense of individual and unit

superiority. Next, he needed a larger battle in which he could numerically overpower the enemy.

The Akyab offensive of the first Arakan campaign was supposed to be that victory.[54] However,

since Slim was not yet the Army commander, his predecessor insisted on using the same tactics

employed in the 1942 campaign with no better results.

Slim was undaunted, however, and after he assumed command of the Fourteenth Army,

he arranged the battle that would enable him to defeat a large Japanese force and dispel the myth

---

[49] Slim, 118.

[50] Ibid., 118.

[51] Ibid., 181. Slim notes, "…rumors were assiduously spread picturing the Japanese as the super bogy-men of the jungle, harping on their savagery, their superior equipment and training, the hardships our men suffered, the lack of everything, the faults in our leadership, and the general hopelessness of expecting ever to defeat the enemy."

[52] Ibid., 188.

[53] Ibid., 189.

[54] Ibid., 150-151. Slim indicates that the Akyab offensive was supposed to "wipe out the last four months of defeat and frustration," but the resulting failure caused a significant decline in morale."

of Japanese invincibility. As the Fourteenth Army trained along the India-Burma border, Slim learned that the Japanese planned to exploit their success in first Arakan campaign by continuing their offensive after the monsoons ended. Their plan was to destroy the British Fifteenth Corps and occupy Chittagong, India to set the stage for a Japanese invasion of India.[55] Slim viewed this as an opportunity to mass his own forces, to fight on ground of his choosing, and to exploit the enemy's overly optimistic planning. After several tense situations, Slim's army soundly defeated the Japanese forces. Slim notes, "it was the first time we had won a battle on a spot where we had previously lost one…" and he saw it as the turning point in the Burma campaign.[56] Thus, Slim's challenge to his organization's thinking that the British could not fight and win in the jungle against the Japanese was successful.[57] His organization now knew it could.

Slim also challenged the organization's thinking in its reliance on motor transportation and supplies. He believed that the British Army was overly reliant on motorized transportation and had untenable expectations for supply.[58] He felt that this road tether was one of the greatest factors contributing to the 1942 campaign defeat.[59] Additionally, he noted, "They (the Japanese) launched their troops into the boldest offensives on the slenderest administrative margins; our training was all against this. The British Army…tended to stress supply at the expense of mobility."[60] Slim realized that for his forces to fight and win in the jungle, they must significantly reduce their reliance on motor transportation which bound them to the limited road networks in

---

[55] Slim, 237. The Japanese commander's plan called for his forces to destroy the British Fifteenth Corps and seize Chittagong within ten days.

[56] Ibid., 245-246.

[57] Ibid., 247. Slim notes, "The legend of the Japanese invincibility in the jungle, so long fostered by so many who should have known better, was smashed."

[58] Ibid., 29.

[59] Ibid., 29. Slim noted, "Nearly all our transport was mechanical, and this stretched our columns for miles along a single road through the jungle, vulnerable everywhere from air and ground …It made us fight on a narrow front, while the enemy, moving wide through the jungle, encircled us and placed a force behind us across the only road… this being tied to a road proved our undoing."

[60] Ibid., 539.

Burma, and that they must learn to live on much less than a typical British force was accustomed to receiving in supplies.

The first thing Slim did to challenge his organization's reliance on motorized transportation was to take it away from them. Even during the retreat, he reorganized his transport situation by forcing infantry brigades to rely partly on pack animals, and by taking all but the most essential divisional transportation assets away from them. It resulted in greater flexibility to attack the enemy's flanks.[61] He continued this trend in his training before the counteroffensive. In one instance, a newly assigned unit concentrated all of its motor transport along the main road in a village, which Japanese air forces subsequently attacked. Slim noted, "Relieved of this transport, the division found, like others in Burma, that it could move faster and more freely without it."[62] By challenging his unit's reliance on motor transportation, Slim eliminated the tether to the limited road network and enabled his units to maneuver through the jungles as the Japanese did during the 1942 campaign.

In logistics, Slim challenged the organization's thinking on the amount of supplies necessary to sustain combat units. Slim observed that the Japanese moved easily through the jungle because they traveled light and lived off the country.[63] He reasoned that if British forces reduced their reliance on motorized transport, a similar cut in supply rates would accompany it. In fact, a lack of roads, aircraft, and the supplies themselves forced Slim to reduce his organization's dependence on them. Slim notes, "With us, necessity was truly the mother of invention."[64] Slim cut the four hundred tons considered a normal level of supply for a division down to one hundred and twenty without decreasing efficiency or morale.[65] Additionally,

---

[61] Slim, 51-52.

[62] Ibid., 318.

[63] Ibid., 29.

[64] Ibid., 540.

[65] Ibid., 540.

reduced availability of supplies forced his units to be innovative.[66] One example was the invention of the "parajute," which was a substitution for a parachute made entirely out of jute.[67] This invention enabled Slim to make up for an inadequate supply of aerial re-supply parachutes and allowed him to reduce his dependence on the road network. By challenging his organization's thinking on the amount of supplies required and the methods for sustaining his combat units, Slim enabled his organization to overcome the extreme lack of supplies and equipment that hampered the Burma Army during the 1942 defeat.

Alternative Analysis:

Additionally, Slim incorporated alternative analysis into his decision-making. He used alternative analysis to redefine his unit's use of air assets for movement, re-supply, and treatment of casualties. During the 1942 campaign, the Burma Army suffered from an extreme shortage of all types of supplies, including air assets. Not only were the aircraft and supplies simply unavailable due to priorities in other theaters, but the Japanese maintained complete air superiority for the entire campaign. To make matter worse, the Japanese employed "hook" and "road-block" tactics that cut off British supply routes and caused severe shortages of reinforcements, ammunition, and supplies.[68] This supply crisis forced the British Army to focus on reopening roads instead of focusing on regaining the initiative or building a strong defense to stop the Japanese advance.

Slim realized that the battlefield conditions during his counteroffensive would be similar, and that he could not rely on the road network if he hoped to employ envelopment tactics similar to the Japanese methods. He had to have an alternate plan for moving and sustaining his combat

---

[66] Slim, 540. He notes, "We learnt that if the spirit could be made willing the flesh would do without many things and that quick brains and willing hands could, from the meager resources, produce astonishing results."

[67] Ibid., 225.

[68] Ibid., 119. These shortages exacerbated the miserable conditions the soldiers endured during the long retreat.

units. He concluded that he could move and sustain large formations entirely by air, which greatly increased his options for employing forces away from road networks and deep in enemy territory. Of course, this capability depended entirely upon availability of air assets and the Royal Air Force regaining air superiority over Burma. The RAF quickly achieved and maintained air superiority, but Slim struggled for the entire counteroffensive to acquire enough air assets to move and sustain his forces. [69] Employing this air transport strategy, however, required a transformation in how his organization viewed aerial support.

To effect this transformation, Slim started with the notion that air movement was the same as any other type of movement.[70] By incorporating air movement and aerial re-supply into his training regimen and by forcing his commanders to use it during operations, Slim changed his unit's mindset about employing air assets. Moving and sustaining his troops by air became second nature. Slim notes, "To us, all this was as normal as moving or maintaining troops by railway or road, and that attitude of mind was, I suppose, one of our main reformations."[71] This "airmindedness" as Slim calls it, was unprecedented in Army organizations at the time.[72] During the second Chindit expedition in March 1944, Slim landed thirty thousand men and five thousand animals well behind Japanese lines, and sustained them for several months. Slim states this was the largest airborne operation of the entire war.[73] Slim's alternative analysis of employing air

---

[69] Slim, 545.

[70] Ibid., 165. Slim notes, "We approached the problem from the starting point that transportation by air was no more extraordinary than movement by road, rail, or boat; it was merely one method of moving things and men."

[71] Ibid., 544.

[72] Ibid. 165. Slim uses the term "airmindedness" to denote the view that aircraft are simply a vehicle. He states that if you view it as anything else, (i.e. a weapon), you are not "airminded."

[73] Ibid., 544. The Chindits, also known as the 3rd Indian Division, were a special operations force organized by Brigadier General Orde Wingate, designed to conduct operations against enemy targets deep in enemy territory. It was composed of British, Burmese, African, and Gurkha soldiers. The first Chindit expedition occurred during the First Arakan campaign after the long retreat in 1942 in an effort to disrupt Japanese communications. Slim's assessment of this first Chindit expedition was that it was very costly in men and material in return for the resources in men and materiel it required. However, he praised it for its

assets to move and sustain his forces enabled him to employ forces deep in enemy territory over long periods.

Another mental transformation Slim affected in his unit was the perception of the army's role in using air assets for moving and sustaining Army units. Slim learned early on in his career that close coordination between the air arm and the ground arm was important.[74] From the moment Slim took command of Fifteenth Corps, which continued during his tenure as Fourteenth Army Commander, Slim insisted that the Air Command headquarters was collocated with his headquarters.[75] This ensured a unity of effort in planning and executing operations.

Additionally, he changed the attitude prevailing at the time that air operations were solely the purview of the air arm.[76] Slim knew that air movement and re-supply required a significant investment in time and resources by ground forces, especially on the scale he anticipated in his counteroffensive.[77] He put his organization to work assisting the air arm in planning and executing air movement and supply operations throughout the campaign. Had Slim left planning and execution of air support exclusively to the air arm, it is doubtful that his forces would have

---

psychological benefit it provided to the British forces. The raid succeeded in penetrating deep behind Japanese lines and returned home. Slim exploited the expedition for its propaganda value in showing that British forces had bested the Japanese in jungle fighting. The second Chindit expedition was part of Slim's counteroffensive into Burma, and the Chindit expedition's part of the campaign was to cut the Japanese line of communication in the Northern Corps area (Stillwell), and to help the American-Chinese advance.

[74] Slim, 9. Slim states, "sixteen months before...I had learnt a sharp lesson on the necessity for the headquarters of the land forces and of the air forces supporting them to be together."

[75] Ibid., 132. When Slim assumed command of Fifteenth Corps, he found that his headquarters was collocated with the Air Operations Command, responsible for Burma and East India. Slim was responsible only for Burma, and he recognized that the A.O.C. should have collocated with Eastern Army. However, he capitalized on the close proximity and developed an atmosphere of close cooperation that remained for the duration of the counteroffensive.

[76] Ibid., 545. Slim asserts that the prevailing attitude of ground forces was that the only requirements for air operations were "aircraft and men to fly and maintain them."

[77] Ibid., 545. He states, "The organization of air supply is as much a job for the army as for the air force." Additionally he states, "It was quite easy theoretically to demonstrate that what we were doing was impossible to continue of any length of time. Yet the skill, courage and devotion of the airmen, British and American, both in the air an don the ground, combined with the hard work and organizing ability of the soldiers, not only did it, but kept on doing it month after month."

succeeded in the critical battles of the counteroffensive, and the overall campaign might well have ended in failure.

Finally, Slim incorporated alternative analysis in addressing the severe medical challenges caused by the environmental conditions and battle. During the 1942 campaign, the Burma Corps suffered an exceedingly high level of non-battle casualties from disease. Dysentery and Malaria decimated British forces during the long retreat, and disease caused one hundred and twenty casualties for every soldier wounded in battle.[78] Since reinforcements were not forthcoming, he knew he needed a better system for treating disease casualties. Slim based his strategy on prevention, treating casualties forward, and using air evacuation.

During the 1942 Burma campaign, British forces in Burma held the lowest priority for supplies, materiel and men. Slim knew that there would be no change in this low priority during his 1945 counteroffensive, so he developed a plan to prevent the high level of casualties experienced during the 1942 campaign. Instead of focusing his efforts on acquiring more medical personnel and supplies, he focused on prevention.[79] His plan for preventing sickness included applying the latest medical research, and improving discipline.

Several advances in the treatment of tropical diseases in the early 1940's aided Slim in reducing casualties during the 1945 campaign. These treatments included sulphonamide compounds, penicillin, mepacrine, and DDT. Due to supply challenges, these treatments were simply unavailable during the 1942 campaign. Even in the 1945 campaign, Slim's men benefited from these new treatments later than he would have liked, but early enough to save many lives.[80]

---

[78] Slim, 177.

[79] Ibid., 178. He states, "It was no use waiting for others to come to our help. Nor was it much use trying to increase our hospital accommodation. Prevention was better than cure. We had to stop men going sick, or, if they went sick, from staying sick."

[80] Ibid., 178.

More important than these new treatments, however, Slim realized that good discipline, enforced by his regimental officers, was critical to preventing the tropical diseases that crippled his army in the 1942 campaign.[81] These regimental officers ensured the men used preventative medication and enforced clothing regulations designed to prevent disease. Additionally, the regimental officers ensured the men quickly treated minor cuts and scrapes and ensured they adhered to personal hygiene standards. Slim's focus on discipline to prevent disease had a dramatic effect. In 1943, the sickness rate for the Fourteenth Army was twelve per thousand per day, which equated to one hundred and twenty sickness casualties for every man wounded.[82] Eighty-four percent per year of Slim's men acquired malaria.[83] Slim realized that sickness would quickly evaporate his combat power if he did not do something to reduce it. While results from Slim's methods did not appear quickly, by 1945 Slim notes that the sickness rate for the entire Fourteenth Army was one per thousand per day.[84]

Another method Slim applied to reduce the impact of disease and sickness on his forces was to treat casualties forward. During the 1942 campaign, the British army treated diseases by evacuating patients all the way to India.[85] Due to the horrendous road conditions and overburdened lines of communication, this evacuation often resulted in five months before the patient returned to duty in Burma.[86] While the propensity to acquire these diseases was high, Slim also faced a tendency for soldiers to contract malaria intentionally so that they could escape

---

[81] Slim, 180. Slim states, "Good doctors are no use without good discipline. More than half the battle against disease is fought, not by the doctors, but by the regimental officers."

[82] Ibid., 177.

[83] Ibid., 177.

[84] Ibid., 180.

[85] Ibid., 178. Slim notes, "Up to now, when a man contracted malaria, he had been transported, while his disease was at its height, in great discomfort hundreds of miles by road, rail, and boat to a hospital in India."

[86] Ibid., 178. Slime notes that many times, the patient never returned to Burma as the Far East Command found other jobs in India for them.

the horrors of the front lines.[87] Given the exceptionally high rate of disease and the lack of

reinforcements coming forward, Slim had to develop a plan to treat these casualties forward in

order to reduce the strain on his combat power.

To solve the disease problem, Slim developed Malaria Forward Treatment Units

(MFTUs).[88] These treatment units were field hospitals that operated a few miles behind the front

lines, which treated disease patients within twenty-four hours of contracting the disease.

Generally, a patient could recover and return to duty on the front lines in about three weeks

instead of several months, which greatly reduced the strain on combat power in forward units.[89]

In addition, these MFTUs significantly reduced the strain on already overburdened lines of

communication, decreased the patient's discomfort endured over the long trip to India, and

reduced the incidence of soldiers trying to escape the front lines by contracting malaria or other

diseases.

Finally, Slim incorporated alternative analysis into casualty evacuation. In the 1942

campaign, the British army transported wounded and sick casualties entirely by road, rail, and

boat. Slim realized that air evacuation could reduce the discomfort of patients, reduce time away

from the front lines, and save lives of the seriously wounded or sick. While air assets in the 1942

campaign were severely limited, they began to increase as the counteroffensive approached. Slim

took advantage of the increase by developing a system of air evacuation to transport casualties

from the front lines to intermediate field hospitals, and all the way back to India if required.[90]

---

[87] Slim, 179.

[88] Ibid., 178.

[89] Ibid., 178.

[90] Ibid., 180. Speaking of the effectiveness of his intermediate field hospitals, Slim notes, "One such hospital took in during 1944 and 1945 over eleven thousand British casualties straight from the front line. The total deaths in that hospital were twenty-three. Air evacuation did more in the Fourteenth Army to save lives than any other agency."

Using this method, wounded soldiers requiring life saving surgery often arrived at the hospitals within several hours. The old method would take days to reach the same location.

Alternative Perspectives:

In addition to challenging the organization's thinking and incorporating alternative analysis, Slim incorporated alternative perspectives into his decision-making. Before arriving in Burma for the first time, Slim realized that he knew nothing about the enemy he would face there. He notes, "I reflected also how very ignorant I was of the Japanese, their methods, and their commanders."[91] To make up for his ignorance, Slim sought the perspectives of others who had fought the Japanese before, and the perspectives of the Japanese commanders he faced.

He found one such perspective in a Chinese general who he met upon arrival in Burma. Slim knew that this Chinese general played a large part in the only Chinese victory against Japanese forces up to that point, and he was the only Allied commander Slim knew of that had actually defeated the Japanese in battle.[92] Capitalizing on the opportunity to make himself smarter on his new enemy, he talked with the Chinese general at length about the Japanese methods. He learned that the Japanese rarely planned for delays or had contingency plans in case their plan did not unfold as envisioned."[93] Slim used this perspective to develop his theory that disruptions in the Japanese plan would cause their entire plan to fall apart, and he based his tactics and overall campaign plan on this perspective.

Slim also incorporated his understanding of the Japanese perspective into his decision-making. In planning for the counteroffensive, Slim believed he knew a little about the Japanese intentions, but he realized that he knew very little about their reserve forces and almost nothing at

---

[91] Slim, 20.

[92] Ibid., 18.

[93] Ibid., 18. Slim states, "His experience was that the Japanese, confident in their own prowess, frequently attacked on a very small administrative margin of safety. He estimated that a Japanese force would usually not have more than nine days' supplies available. If you could hold the Japanese for that time, prevent them capturing your supplies, and then counter-attack them, you would destroy them."

all about the Japanese commanders opposing him.[94] However, Slim studied the Russo-Japanese war, and developed an understanding of how the Japanese generals would behave based on their experience there. He knew that during that war, the Russians lost every battle without committing their reserves. The Japanese, on the other hand, always committed every soldier in reserve in order to achieve victory. Slim reasoned that lessons of the Russo-Japanese war shaped the tendencies of the Japanese commanders he faced, and he sought to exploit those lessons to his advantage.[95]

Additionally, Slim incorporated Japanese perspective in his decision-making by exploiting their assumption that British forces would respond to their "hook" and "road-block" tactics in the same way as during the 1942 campaign.[96] However, Slim had accustomed his forces to fighting with enemy forces behind them, and they did not react the way the Japanese expected. In the first Arakan campaign, the Japanese attack faltered, and as expected, the Japanese commander committed all of his reserves to achieve his objective. In the end, he failed. Slim used the Japanese perspective to turn the tables on the Japanese commanders and win a major battle against Japanese forces.[97] By incorporating the Japanese perspective into his plan, Slim baited the Japanese into giving him the decisive battle he needed prior to the

---

[94] Slim, 221. Slim states, "we knew something of the Japanese intentions, but little of the dispositions of their reserves, and practically nothing about one of the most important factors that a general has to consider – the character of the opposing commanders."

[95] Ibid., 221. He states, "The Japanese generals we were fighting had been brought up on the lessons of that war, and all I had seen of them in this convinced me that they would run true to form and hold back nothing." Additionally, he states, "I could only expect him [the Japanese commander opposing Slim] to be, like most Japanese commanders I had met, a bold tactical planner of offensive movements, completely confident in the superiority of his troops, and prepared to use his last reserves rather than abandon a plan."

[96] Ibid., 237. Speaking of his understanding of the Japanese perspective of likely British reactions to Japanese tactics, which he acquired from captured Japanese documents containing their plan to seize Chittagong during the second Arakan battle, he states, "The basic idea was the British divisions, when thus cut off, would behave as they had in the past, and, deprived of all supplies, turn to fight their way back to clear their communications."

[97] Ibid., 246. In Slim's view, this first victory over the Japanese was the turning point in the Burma campaign.

counteroffensive, which set the conditions for Slim to have sufficient force ratios to achieve success during the counteroffensive.

Another example of Slim incorporating the Japanese perspective into his decision-making occurred during planning for the second decisive battle of the counteroffensive. Slim's original conception of how the Japanese would fight this second battle proved wrong, but he adjusted and incorporated the Japanese perspective into his adjusted plan, which enabled him to achieve victory. Slim needed the Japanese to fight another decisive battle on ground favorable to the British. He wanted a decisive battle to occur on the Shwebo Plain between the Irrawaddy and Chindwin Rivers because it was more open and accessible to tanks and air support than the predominant jungle terrain throughout most of Burma. For these reasons, the Shwebo Plain was disadvantageous for the Japanese to defend. However, Slim believed the Japanese would defend there because of the mentality of the Japanese commanders. [98] Unfortunately, General Kimura proved to be an atypical Japanese commander, and Slim's assumption that he would behave the same as the others was erroneous. Kimura was much more realistic, and he completely recast the defense plan for central Burma and defended behind the Irrawaddy instead of in front of it. [99]

Although Slim's original conception of the Japanese plan proved wrong, he recovered by using these same Japanese perspectives and applying them to the Japanese defense behind the Irrawaddy. Slim then developed a plan that assumed the Japanese would commit the bulk of their forces against a feint towards Mandalay, which Slim believed the Japanese viewed as critical to holding central Burma. This deception would enable Slim's main effort to cross the Irrawaddy unopposed, seize Meiktila, which was more crucial to British plans, and envelop the bulk of the

---

[98] Slim, 380. Slim states, "I expected him to conform to type, to be over-bold, inflexible, and reluctant to change a plan once made. <Kimura> would be confident that he could beat me on his own ground and, even if he were not, he would never dare to lose face by giving up territory without a struggle. He would see the Chindwin behind us, not the Irrawaddy behind him."

[99] Ibid., 391.

Japanese forces. Slim believed that the local Japanese commander, General Katamura, would commit all of his forces to Mandalay piecemeal, which would allow Slim to defeat Japanese divisions sequentially rather than simultaneously. As expected, Katamura counterattacked with a sizeable force where he believed the main British attack was occurring, to Mandalay, but he misread the situation and committed his forces piecemeal.[100] Ultimately, the Japanese clung stubbornly to their defenses as Slim expected, and their piecemeal commitment of counterattack forces enabled Slim to destroy the bulk of Japanese forces in Burma and set the stage for the seizure of Rangoon.

The dire circumstances under which Slim assumed command of the Fourteenth Army, the posturing of the Japanese forces to continue their invasion into India, and the extremely low priority of supplies, materiel and men afforded to Burma seemed to preclude any hope that a counteroffensive into Burma would be successful. However, Slim overcame the seemingly insurmountable odds by challenging the organizations thinking, incorporating alternative analysis and incorporating alternative perspectives into his decision-making. Slim challenged the organization's thinking in the areas of the British capability to fight in the jungle and their over reliance on motor transportation and supplies. He incorporated alternative analysis to redefine his unit's use of air assets for movement, re-supply, and their treating casualties. In addition, he incorporated Chinese and Japanese perspectives into his decision-making to develop a better understanding of the Japanese mindset, which he then effectively used against them by predicting how the Japanese commanders would fight key battles. By applying the core concepts of red teaming, Slim turned the tables on the Japanese and destroyed the Japanese forces in Burma.

---

[100] Slim, 415. Slim notes, "Katamura…instead of building up a strong, well-prepared attack, committed the common Japanese error of launching his troops into the assault piecemeal as they arrived."

Case Study 2: T.E. Lawrence in WWI

Another example of effectively incorporating red teaming core concepts into decision-making is T.E. Lawrence during the Arab Revolt against the Turks in World War I. Similar to Sir William Slim in Burma, T.E. Lawrence improved his decision-making by challenging the organization's thinking, incorporating alternative analysis, and incorporating alternative perspectives.

The Arab Revolt against the Turks in World War I began in June of 1916. The evolution of the revolt lay in British desires to knock Turkey out of the war, which would enable them to focus their efforts on Germany.[101] Amid British assurances of help, poorly armed and inexperienced Arab tribesman conducted a surprise attack on Turkish garrisons in Medina and Mecca.[102] Not surprisingly, their attack failed, and the Arab forces then conducted a blockade of the Medina and Mecca garrisons. Eventually, the Turks transitioned to offensive operations forcing the Arab forces to withdraw into the hills about fifty miles south-west along the road to Mecca, where the Arab revolt stagnated and the Turks prepared to "crush the revolt where it had started" in Mecca.[103]

At this point in the campaign, the British plan for the Arab forces was to conduct a delay with Feisal's tribesman in order to slow the Turkish advance on Mecca and allow time for Sherif Ali, Feisal's oldest brother, to build an Arab regular army in Rabegh. British advisors believed that Arab tribesman could never defeat Turkish forces by defending the hills, which necessitated developing an Arab regular force to defend Rabegh.

---

[101] T.E. Lawrence, *Seven Pillars of Wisdom* (Harmondsworth, Middlesex, England: Penguin Books, Ltd.,1926), 26. Lawrence states, "Some Englishmen…believed that a rebellion of Arabs against Turks would enable England, while fighting Germany, simultaneously to defeat her ally Turkey."

[102] T.E. Lawrence, "The Evolution of a Revolt," Army Quarterly and Defence Journal (October 1920), 1.

[103] Ibid., 1.

Under these conditions, T.E. Lawrence entered the picture. He went to Arabia to determine the feasibility of building the Arab Regular Army and if Feisal's men could hold in the hills long enough to enable Sharif Ali to do so. His initial assessment was that Feisal's men could hold the Turks indefinitely. He states, "They were posted in hills and defiles of such natural strength that it seemed to me very improbable that the Turks could force them out, just by their superior numbers."[104] However, the Turkish forces attacked and quickly broke through Feisal's defense, creating a crisis for the British plan to defeat the Turks and Germans simultaneously, as well as for the budding Arab Revolt.

Given these dire circumstances, Lawrence decided that the only hope left was to threaten the Turkish flanks and thereby force the Turks into a defensive posture to deal with the threat. He felt that the Arab tribesman could capitalize on this threat by moving toward the Hejaz railway north of Medina, thereby forcing the Turks into a defensive posture along the railway and allowing the Arab forces to regain the initiative.[105] The Turks responded by moving their forces back to Medina, and further splitting their force to protect Medina and guard the railway simultaneously. Unknown to Lawrence at the time, this move to Wejh proved to be the turning point for the Arab revolt. For the duration of the war, Feisal's tribesmen continually harassed the Hejaz railway and captured cut off Turkish garrisons.

This turn around and subsequent success of the Arab revolt is remarkable. Although Lawrence laments the fact that the Arab revolt did not capture Damascus on its own merit, this "sideshow of a sideshow" proved to be a key factor that enabled General Allenby to succeed.[106]

---

[104] Lawrence 1920, 3.

[105] Ibid., 4. Lawrence states, "…if we moved towards the Hejaz railway behind Medina, we might stretch our threat (and accordingly, their flank) as far, potentially, as Damascus, eight hundred miles away to the North."

[106] Ibid., 21. Lawrence states, "…we were able eventually to reduce the Turks to helplessness, and complete victory seemed to be almost within our sight when General Allenby by his immense stroke in Palestine threw the enemy's main forces into hopeless confusion and put an immediate end to the Turkish war. We were very happy to have done with all our pains, but sometimes since I have felt a private regret

By applying the core concepts of red teaming, Lawrence led a ragged and undisciplined army of tribesmen in systematically defeating the Turkish army in the Hejaz. First, Lawrence challenged the thinking of the British command in Egypt and the leaders of the Arab revolt by re-evaluating the capabilities of the Arab irregular forces. Second, he incorporated alternative analysis into decision-making through re-evaluating the Turkish threat in Medina, the strengths of the Arab and Turkish forces, and the tactics the Arabs should use in attacking the Turkish lines of communication. This analysis evolved into an alternative theory of irregular warfare. Finally, and most importantly, he incorporated the perspectives of the Arabs and the Turks into his analysis, which enabled him to apply his new theory of irregular warfare to the Arab revolt.

Challenging the Organization's Thinking:

When Lawrence first arrived in Arabia, the common conception of warfare based on the theories of Clausewitz, Jomini and Foch shaped his beliefs about the capabilities of the Arab irregular forces and the course of action the British and Arab forces should pursue. Conventional wisdom dictated that the only way to win in war was to engage and defeat the enemy in battle. Lawrence states, "We were obsessed by the dictum of Foch that the ethic of modern war is to seek for the enemy's army, his centre [sic] of power, and destroy it in battle."[107] Based on this type of thinking, Lawrence believed that Arab tribesmen alone could not win their revolt against the Turks, so they needed an Arab regular force.[108]

While Lawrence did not believe that the irregulars could attack a fixed point successfully, he did believe they could successfully defend a fixed point. Based on this belief, when Lawrence made his initial reconnaissance of Feisal's tribesmen in their defensive position south of Medina,

---

that his too-greatness deprived me of the opportunity of following to the end the dictum of Saxe that a war might be won without fighting battles." General Allenby used the Arab Revolt as a shaping effort in his campaign to defeat Turkish forces in Palestine.

[107] Lawrence 1920, 3.

[108] Ibid., 3. He states, "…we all looked only to the regulars to win the war…Irregulars would not attack positions and so they seemed to us incapable of forcing a decision."

he believed that they could delay the Turkish forces from reaching Rabegh indefinitely if the British provided light machine guns and advisors. However, contrary to Lawrence's hypothesis, the Turks broke through Feisal's defense easily, and Lawrence realized that the irregular forces could not defend a fixed point either.[109]

The success of the Turks in pushing through Feisal's defense south of Rabegh placed the entire Arab revolt in jeopardy, and the resulting emergency forced Lawrence to reconsider his conception about the capabilities of the Arab irregulars. After some quick thinking about the current situation and the events that led up to that point, he realized that the Turks were initially hesitant to attack south out of Medina, which they could have done much earlier than they did, precisely because of the threat the Arab irregulars posed to their flanks if they moved south. He realized that the strength of the Arab irregulars was not massing and slugging it out with the Turks, but their ability to pose a constant, elusive threat along the Turkish lines of communication.[110]

The Turkish flank extended from their front line just north of Rabegh to Medina, a distance of only fifty miles. Yet, the threat the Arabs posed to it caused the Turks considerable anxiety and resulted in hesitation to attack south to recapture Mecca. Lawrence realized that the irregular threat could extend much farther north because the Turkish line of communication along the Hejaz railway, linking the forces in Medina to Turkish forces in Syria, was vulnerable in the same way.[111] By threatening the Turkish lines of communication so far north, he believed that

---

[109] Lawrence 1920, 3. He states, "...they proved to us the second theorem of irregular war – namely, that irregular troops are as unable to defend a point or line as they are to attack it."

[110] Ibid., 4. He states, "...it occurred to me that perhaps the virtue of irregulars lay in depth, not in face, and that it had been the threat of attack by them upon the Turkish northern flank which had made the enemy hesitate for so long."

[111] Ibid., 4. He states, "...if we moved towards the Hejaz railway behind Medina, we might stretch our threat as far, potentially, as Damascus, eight hundred miles away to the north."

the Turks would have to revert to a defensive posture and the Arab revolt might survive and even regain the initiative.[112]

Since there was no other way to save the situation in accordance with the existing conception of building an Arab regular, Lawrence convinced Feisal of his new conception. Lawrence needed to test his new hypothesis, so they marched Feisal's tribesman to Wejh, well north of Medina, and put themselves in a position to threaten the Hejaz railway.[113] He states, "This eccentric movement acted like a charm."[114] The Turks immediately abandoned their offensive to retake Mecca and recalled their forces all the way back to Medina. Further, they split their force in half so that they could protect Medina and guard the Hejaz railway simultaneously.[115]

Armed with this new understanding of the value of irregular forces, and the impact they had on the Turks by simply moving to Wejh and attacking the Hejaz railway, Lawrence was able to challenge the thinking of the British command in Egypt and the Arab leaders. The existing conception was that irregular forces lacked the capability to defeat the Turkish army because they could not fight a conventional battle. Based on this, the British command and the Arab leaders thought they required a force of Arab regulars. Lawrence's success with Feisal's men in putting the Turks on the defensive and disrupting their line of communication changed the thinking of both organizations. Feisal and the other Arab leaders realized that the Arab irregulars were the backbone of the revolt and could achieve victory even without a regular Arab force. The British command in Egypt realized that the Arab tribesmen were successful in tying down a large part of

---

[112] Lawrence 1926, 116. Lawrence states, "Such a move would force the Turks to the defensive, and we might regain the initiative."

[113] Ibid., 116. Lawrence states, "We decided that to regain the initiative we must ignore the main body of the enemy, and concentrate far off on his railway flank. The first step towards this was to move our base to Wejh."

[114] Lawrence 1920, 4.

[115] Ibid., 4.

the Turkish forces in Arabia, which enabled the British to achieve the force ratios necessary for General Allenby to move on Palestine and force Turkey out of the war.

Alternative Analysis:

Challenging the organization's thinking often involves incorporating alternative analysis to arrive at a new conception that is contrary to the existing thinking. Lawrence used alternative analysis to crystallize his conception of the capabilities, tactics, and strategy for the Arab revolt. After establishing a base in Wejh, and while on the way to coordinate a counterattack on Medina with the other Arab leaders, Lawrence became ill and spent ten days recovering in a tent. During this illness, Lawrence took advantage of the time to rethink his conception of the Arab revolt, and conducted his own alternative analysis, which he used to challenge the organization's thinking. This alternative analysis consisted of re-evaluating the threat the Turks posed by occupying Medina, the aims of each side, and the tactics the Arab irregulars should use in attacking the Turkish lines of communication.

As described earlier, when Lawrence and Feisal led the Arab tribesman to Wejh, the Turks responded by abandoning their attack on Mecca and established a defense of Medina and the railway. The British command in Egypt and the Arab leaders viewed this as an opportunity to conduct a conventional attack using the Arab regular force against Medina. However, the thinking Lawrence did while sick convinced him that pushing the Turks out of Medina was exactly the wrong thing to do because Turkish forces tied down in Medina was actually beneficial to the Arab revolt. After recovering from his illness, Lawrence went back to Wejh to convince the British command to abandon the attack on Medina, but to no avail. He states, "They preferred the limited and direct objective of Medina."[116]

---

[116] Lawrence 1926, 170.

Lawrence realized that before the move to Wejh, Medina was valuable to the Turks because it provided them with a base from which to stage their assault on Mecca. However, the move to Wejh changed the posture of the Turks to the defensive, and further reduced the size of the garrison in Medina to a point where it was incapable of significant offensive action because the Turks had to protect the railway as well. Further, the disruption of the Hejaz railway prevented the Turks from reinforcing or providing supplies to the Medina garrison.[117]

In Arab hands, Medina would not be as effective a base for the Arab forces as Rabegh or Wejh because it was not on the coast and British supply ships could not provide supplies and equipment as they were to the coastal bases. Additionally, it posed no direct threat to the base areas the Arabs were currently using. In Lawrence's new analysis, Medina was worthless to the Arab forces and he could not see value in attacking to retake it. He states, "We had taken away their power to harm us, and yet wanted to take away their town."[118] The result of this analysis was that Lawrence believed the Turks had taken themselves out of the war by clinging to Medina after the Arabs moved to Wejh.[119]

Next, Lawrence analyzed the aims of the Arab and the Turkish forces. He determined that the aim of the Arabs was to expel the Turks from Arabic speaking lands because they could only have liberty after achieving this goal.[120] Killing Turkish soldiers was extraneous to this

---

[117] Lawrence 1926, 194. Lawrence states, "Its (Medina) harmfulness had been patent when we were at Yenbo and the Turks in it were going to Mecca: but we had changed all that by our march to Wejh. Today we were blockading the railway, and they only defending it. The garrison of Medina, reduced to an inoffensive size, were sitting in trenches destroying their own power of movement by eating the transport they could no longer feed." The disruption of the railway prevented the Turks from supplying the Medina garrison.

[118] Ibid., 194.

[119] Lawrence 1920, 6. He states, "They were harmless sitting there; if we took them prisoner, they would cost us food and guards in Egypt: if we drove them northward into Syria, they would join the main army blocking us in Sinai. On all counts they were best where they were, and they valued Medina and wanted to keep it. Let them!"

[120] Lawrence 1926, 196. He states, "I...saw that their aim was geographical, to extrude the Turk from all Arabic-speaking lands in Asia."

aim. Control of the land was the objective of both the Arab forces and the Turks. The Turks controlled the major cities and the lines of communication linking them, but the Arabs controlled the rest of the countryside. Turkish control of such a limited amount of the Hejaz was insignificant in Lawrence's view.

From here, Lawrence analyzed how each side could control the land, and he realized that all of the odds were in the Arab's favor. He estimated the total land area of the Arabic speaking lands to be about one hundred and forty thousand square miles.[121] Given this huge land area, he realized that the Turks could not defend the entire territory if the Arabs did not give them a linear battle.[122] He further calculated that the Turks would have to place a fortified post consisting of at least twenty soldiers every four square miles to defend the entire territory, and the total forces required would be about six hundred thousand, of which they only had one hundred thousand.[123] Since the Arab population was sympathetic to the Arab revolt, the Arabs could control all the territory that the Turks were not currently occupying.[124]

Next, Lawrence analyzed the tactics the Arab irregulars should use in attacking the Turkish lines of communication.   Given the value of the individual Arab tribesman, stemming from their casualty aversion and close tribal and family connections, he realized that he must identify the element most valuable to the Turkish army and pursue that as his goal of destruction. The Turks were certainly not casualty averse, as they sometimes sacrificed soldiers for almost no gain. Additionally, they could regenerate forces easily in Syria or Turkey. Resources, on the

---

[121] Lawrence 1920, 7.

[122] Ibid., 7. Lawrence states, "…how would the Turks defend all that…no doubt by a trench line across the bottom, if we were an army attacking with banners displayed…but suppose we were an influence (as we might be), an idea, a thing invulnerable, intangible, without front or back, drifting about like a gas…a regular soldier might be helpless without a target. He would own the ground he sat on, and what he could poke his rifle at."

[123] Lawrence 1926, 198.

[124] Ibid., 194-195. He states, "Out of every thousand square miles of Hejaz nine hundred and ninety-nine were now free…If we held the rest, the Turks were welcome to the tiny fraction on which they stood…"

other hand, were much less abundant. Based on this analysis, Lawrence changed the focus of the Arab irregulars from attacking Turkish troops to attacking Turkish resources, specifically rail cars, rail lines, and telegraph lines, in order to isolate and starve the dispersed Turkish forces.[125]

Based on this new analysis of the Arab irregular's target for attacks and their aim, Lawrence reconsidered the type of war the Arab revolt would become. His new analysis was that the Arab revolt would be a "war of detachment."[126] Based on this assessment, Lawrence concludes that, contrary to the existing conception, engaging in battles with the enemy was a mistake for the revolt. The best way to defeat the Turks was to never engage them, but methodically disrupt their line of communication.

All of the aforementioned alternative analysis, however, depended entirely on how the Turks responded to it. Lawrence understood that completely cutting off the Hejaz railway would result in the Turks evacuating the Hejaz and consolidating their forces in Syria. Since the overall aim of the Arab revolt, at least in the eyes of the Arabs, was to eject the Turks from the entire Arabic speaking lands, a consolidated Turkish force in Syria would be extremely difficult to dislodge, making the Arab aim untenable. Lawrence believed that the Turks remaining in Medina and dispersing their forces to protect the railway was actually beneficial to the Arabs, so his analysis was that the Arab irregulars should moderate their disruption of the railway.[127]

Lawrence realized that his new conception contradicted the principles of the current body of military thought based on the theories of Foch, Clausewitz and Jomini. He states, "…the

---

[125] Lawrence 1926, 199. Lawrence states, "In Turkey things were scarce and precious, men less esteemed than equipment. Our cue was to destroy, not the Turk's army, but his minerals."

[126] Ibid., 200. Lawrence states, "Most wars were wars of contact. Ours should be a war of detachment. We were to contain the enemy by the silent threat of a vast unknown desert, not disclosing ourselves till we attacked. The attack might be nominal, directed not against him, but against his stuff; so it would not seek either his strength or his weakness, but his most accessible material. In railway cutting it would be usually an empty stretch of rail; and the more empty, the greater the tactical success."

[127] Ibid., 12. He states, "Our ideal was to keep his railway just working, but only just, with the maximum of loss and discomfort to him."

books gave me the aim in war quite pat, 'the destruction of the organized forces of the enemy' by 'the one process battle.' Victory could only be purchased by blood."[128] His analysis contradicted this theory because the Arabs had no organized forces for the Turks to destroy, and the Arabs casualty aversion prevented them from sacrificing themselves. Based on the conventional wisdom, the Arabs should not be winning, but Lawrence knew that they were having a great deal of success. This contradiction forced him to develop an alternative theory of irregular warfare, turning Clausewitz, Jomini and Foch's theories on their heads. Lawrence summarizes his new theory as follows:

> "It seemed to me proven that our rebellion had an unassailable base, guarded not only from attack, but from the fear of attack. It had a sophisticated alien enemy, disposed as an army of occupation in an area greater than could be dominated effectively from fortified posts. It had a friendly population, of which some two in the hundred were active, and the rest quietly sympathetic to the point of not betraying the movements of the minority. The active rebels had the virtues of secrecy and self-control, and the qualities of speed, endurance and independence of arteries of supply. They had technical equipment enough to paralyze the enemy's communications. A province would be won when we had taught the civilians in it to die for our ideal of freedom. The presence of the enemy was secondary. Final victory seemed certain, if the war lasted long enough for us to work it out."[129]

Lawrence's sickness that immobilized him and confined him in a tent for ten days enabled him to think about the Arab revolt and develop his alternative analysis of irregular warfare and the Arab revolt. His analysis of the threat the Turks posed by occupying Medina, the aims of each side, and the tactics the Arab irregulars should use in attacking the Turkish lines of communication established a new framework for Feisal's tribesmen to operate within. Ultimately, this new framework enabled the Arab revolt to succeed in isolating and destroying the

---

[128] Lawrence 1920, 5.

[129] Lawrence 1926, 202.

Turkish corps occupying the Hejaz, and setting the conditions for General Allenby's attack to seize Palestine.[130]

Alternative Perspectives:

Lawrence's alternative analysis of the Arab revolt resulted in a profoundly different method of warfare that the Arabs used to defeat the Turkish forces in the Hejaz. As stated above, Lawrence developed a theory of rebellion that contradicted the widely subscribed to theories of decisive battles and force on force engagements as necessary to win wars. With this new theory in mind, Lawrence developed strategy and tactics that suited the Arab tribesmen capabilities and nature, and confounded Turkish attempts to counter it in a conventional manner. Both his theory of rebellion and the specific methods he used stemmed from his understanding of the Arabs and Turks. He incorporated the Arab aims for the revolt, his understanding of Arab culture and tribal structure, his understanding of how the Arabs lived and fought, and his understanding of how the Turks would respond to the revolt into his analysis.

The British and Arabs had very different views of the aims of the Arab revolt. In the British conception, the Arab revolt was simply a tool to help the British defeat the Turks while the British simultaneously fought the Germans.[131] This British conception shaped Sir Archibald Murray's plan for the Arabs to attack the Turks in a conventional sense in Medina after Feisal's tribesmen moved to Wejh and threatened the Hejaz railway.[132] Even after the Arabs were

---

[130] Lawrence 1920, 4. Lawrence states, "…when peace came, we had taken thirty-five thousand prisoners, killed and wounded and worn out about as many, and occupied a hundred thousand square miles of the enemy's territory, at little loss to ourselves."

[131] Lawrence 1926, 28. Lawrence states, "I was sent to these Arabs as a stranger, unable to think their thoughts or subscribe their beliefs, but charged by duty to lead them forward and to develop to the highest any movement of theirs profitable to England in her war."

[132] Ibid., 203. Lawrence states, "…It was irksome that he (Sir Archibald Murray) should come butting into our show from Egypt, asking from us alien activities. Yet the British were bigger; and the Arabs lived only by grace of their shadow." Sir Archibald Murray was the commander of British forces in Egypt until General Allenby succeeded him on 27 June 1917.

successful in keeping the Turks in Medina by using Lawrence's tactics, the British still viewed

the Arabs as supporting the British plan to push the Turks out of Syria.

The Arabs, on the other hand, viewed their revolt as a war for freedom. The Turks had

controlled Arabia since the beginning of the Ottoman Empire, when the Caliphate centered itself

in Constantinople. While the Arabs certainly viewed the Turkish Caliphate as illegitimate, it was

of secondary importance in the Arab revolt. Their primary concern was freedom from servitude

to outsiders.[133] From this basis, Lawrence determined that the aim of the Arabs was to expel the

Turks from Arabic speaking lands because they could achieve liberty only after the Turks were

gone.[134] Killing Turkish soldiers was extraneous to this aim. Control of the land was the

objective of both the Arab forces and the Turks.

In addition to understanding the Arab perspective in terms of its aims, Lawrence also

understood the Arab culture and society. Prior to World War I, Lawrence spent years traveling in

Syria and Mesopotamia immersing himself in Arab society. This immersion gave him the ability

to look, as much as possible by an outsider, through the eyes of the Arabs.[135] In addition, he spent

the duration of the war living and fighting with the Arab tribesmen, most of the time in isolation

from any other British or Allied presence. This understanding of the Arab culture and society

enabled him to apply their perspective to his analysis of the Arab revolt and to harness their

strengths towards his ultimate goal of defeating the Turks. He states, "They would follow us, if

we endured with them, and played the game according to their rules." Lawrence spent the entire

---

[133] Lawrence 1926, 197. Lawrence quotes, Emir Abdullah, Feisal's brother, as stating, "…talk of Turkish heresy, or the immoral doctrine of Yeni-Turan, or the illegitimate Caliphate was beside the point. It was Arab country, and the Turks were in it; that was the one issue."

[134] Ibid., 196. He states, "I…saw that their aim was geographical, to extrude the Turk from all Arabic-speaking lands in Asia."

[135] Ibid., 54. Lawrence states, "My poverty had constrained me to mix with the humbler classes, those seldom met by European travelers, and thus my experiences gave me an unusual angle of view, which enabled me to understand and think for the ignorant many as well as for the more enlightened whose rare opinions mattered, not so much for the day, as for the morrow."

war "enduring with them" and he shaped the conception of the Arab revolt into one that fit with their "rules."

The British command in Egypt, on the other had, did not have any Arab cultural knowledge, and Lawrence believed that they could not effectively harness the Arab revolt for England's benefit due to its complexity and their lack of understanding.[136] This lack of cultural knowledge and understanding prevented the British command in Egypt from seeing the inability of the irregular force to conduct conventional operations as anything other than a weakness of leadership and fortitude. Even at the end of the war, most of the British Egyptian Expeditionary Force staff believed that Lawrence's efforts were misguided because they did not conform to the decisive battle theory of warfare. However, since the Arab revolt was a "sideshow of a sideshow," the British command in Egypt gave Lawrence the freedom to test his theory. Had Lawrence remained burdened with the requirement to build an Arab regular force, the Arab revolt would have undoubtedly died in Rabegh and the combined efforts of the Arab revolt and General Allenby might never have ejected the Turks from Syria.

In addition to understanding the Arabs, Lawrence also understood the Turkish perspective and included it in his analysis of the Arab revolt. Before Murray sent Lawrence to Arabia to assess the Arab revolt, Lawrence worked on the intelligence staff of the British Egyptian Expeditionary Force and studied the Turkish army in detail. He knew their order of battle, their tactics, the character of their soldiers, and their thought processes.[137] His understanding of the Turks enabled him to predict how the Turks would react to the new tactics he envisioned for the Arabs. His analysis was that the Turks would try to use conventional methods to deal with Arab revolt because they did not understand the dynamics of rebellion. He

---

[136] Lawrence 1926, 61. Lawrence states, "He (Sir Archibald Murray) could not be entrusted with the Arabian affair; for neither he nor his staff had the ethnological competence needed to deal with so curious a problem."

[137] Ibid., 198. He states, "I knew the Turkish Army exactly..."

states, "They would believe that rebellion was absolute like war, and deal with it on the analogy of war…and war upon rebellion was messy and slow, like eating soup with a knife."[138] He knew that Turkish attempts to deal with the Arab revolt worked in the favor of the Arabs because they would never give the Turks a target to attack.

Lawrence's ability to incorporate the perspectives of the Arabs and the Turks was the most influential aspect of his success in shaping the Arab revolt because the Arab and Turkish perspectives lay at the heart of his analysis. His evaluation of the threat posed by the Turks at Medina, the strengths of the Arab irregular and Turkish forces, and the tactics used by the Arabs all predicated his understanding of Arab and Turkish perspectives. Without this understanding, Lawrence would have continued to subscribe to the prevalent conception of trying to fight the Turks in a conventional battle as the only means to defeat them. His understanding enabled him to see the revolt through the eyes of the Arabs and Turks, and develop an alternate theory of warfare, which he successfully used to defeat the Turks.

Case Study 3: Operation IRAQI FREEDOM

The final case studied presented in this monograph is Operation IRAQI FREEDOM (OIF). The first two case studies demonstrate how challenging the organizational thinking, and incorporating alternative analysis and alternative perspectives into decision making contributed to successful operations by Field Marshal Slim and T.E. Lawrence. Much of the evidence for how Slim and Lawrence used these red teaming concepts and the resulting contribution to their success comes from their own words. In effect, they were their own red team. This case study, in contrast, is a "negative" case study, in that it demonstrates application of red teaming core concepts, but with poor results. OIF is a case study in red teaming gone wrong. It does not focus

---

[138] Lawrence 1926, 198.

exclusively on one military commander, i.e. General Franks, because he did not have the latitude and freedom from interference to plan and execute OIF independently. Field Marshal Slim and T.E. Lawrence had more latitude to conceive and execute their campaigns free from the level of scrutiny General Franks and the CENTCOM staff experienced from their civilian leadership.[139]

While ongoing operations in Iraq five years after the fall of Saddam Hussein's regime indicate that the U.S. certainly has not achieved its strategic objective in the manner envisioned at the outset, the recent "surge" and resulting improvement in the security situation also show that not all is lost.[140] The long-term outcome of OIF is yet undecided. Thus, this case study only demonstrates poor application of the core concepts of red teaming, and how this poor application contributed to CENTCOM's failure to anticipate and prevent the insurgency, terrorism, and sectarian conflicts that developed after Saddam Hussein's regime collapsed.[141]

Contrary to expectations, it would be a mischaracterization to say that none of the core concepts of red teaming surfaced during OIF planning. In fact, one could argue that Secretary Rumsfeld's vision of transforming the U.S. military to one based on speed, agility, and precision is alternative analysis of future warfare requirements. Additionally, the Bush administration's efforts to incorporate the perspective of Iraqi exiles such as Ahmed Chalabi is exactly what the

---

[139] This is not intended as a criticism about the level of involvement of U.S. civilian administrators into planning for war. It is meant only as a reason why this OIF case study is dissimilar to the other two case studies in its lack of focus on an individual military decision maker.

[140] U.S. National Security Council, "National Strategy for Victory in Iraq, November 2005." http://www.whitehouse.gov/infocus/iraq/iraq_strategy_nov2005.html (accessed 8 February, 2008), 3.The strategy defines victory in short, medium, and long-term stages. The long-term definition of victory lists the conditions for victory as "An Iraq that has defeated the terrorists and neutralized the insurgency", "An Iraq that is peaceful, united, stable, democratic, and secure, where Iraqis have the institutions and resources they need to govern themselves justly and provide security for their country," and "An Iraq that is a partner in the global war on terror and the fight against the proliferation of weapons of mass destruction, integrated into the international community, an engine for regional economic growth, and proving the fruits of democratic governance to the region."

[141] Michael Gordon and Trainor, Bernard. *Cobra II: The Inside Story of the Invasion and Occupation of Iraq* (New York: Pantheon Books, Random House Inc., 2006), xxxi. In the Forward, Gordon and Trainor state that they wrote Cobra II to "provide an inside look at how a military campaign that was so successful in toppling Saddam Hussein's regime set the conditions for the insurgency that followed."

red teaming core concept of incorporating alternative perspectives demands. Finally, General

Franks specifically mentions the need to red team his plan during one of his rock drills prior to

initiating OIF.[142] These examples indicate that decision makers made at least a minimal effort to

apply the core concepts of red teaming in their planning for OIF.

However, something obviously went wrong. In *Cobra II*, Gordon and Trainor make the

case that the Bush Administration made errors in planning and executing OIF that directly link

the way the U.S. planned the war to the emergence of the ongoing insurgency.[143] These errors

consist of over-reliance on technology, squelching alternate military and political perspectives,

failing to adapt to battlefield developments, misreading the adversary, and an unrealistic aversion

to nation building. Although some would debate the accuracy of these claims and their impact on

OIF, this case study uses them as a starting point to analyze the use of red teaming core concepts

in planning and execution of OIF. Most of these "errors" are essentially failures or misguided

attempts to apply the red teaming core concepts of incorporating alternative analysis and

alternative perspective into decision-making.

A fundamental precondition of the red team core concepts is that they must exhibit some

degree of realism and accuracy. Rumsfeld's vision that superior intelligence and the ability to

communicate large amounts of data near instantaneously would eliminate the fog of war and

enable a smaller force to achieve decisive results proved false in Iraq. While U.S. forces

---

[142] Gordon and Trainor, 90. Gordon and Trainor state, "Franks added that all of CENTCOM's assumptions should be scrutinized by CIA psychologists and trusted Iraqi defectors. They should 'red team' the briefing slides."

[143] Ibid., 497-498. They state, "...President Bush and his team committed five grievous errors. They underestimated their opponent and failed to understand the welter of ethnic groups and tribes that is Iraq. They did not bring the right tools to the fight and put too much confidence in technology. They failed to adapt to developments on the ground and remained wedded to their prewar analysis even after Iraqis showed their penchant for guerrilla tactics in the first days of the war. They presided over a system in which differing military and political perspectives were discouraged. Finally, they turned their back on the nation-building lessons from the Balkans and other crisis zones and fashioned a plan that unrealistically sought to shift much of the burden onto a defeated and ethnically diverse population and allied nations that were enormously ambivalent about the invasion. Instead of making plans to fight a counterinsurgency, the president and his team drew up plans to bring the troops home and all but declared the war won."

succeeded in quickly crushing all Iraqi conventional forces and toppling the Iraqi regime with a smaller force and fewer casualties than conventional wisdom thought necessary, it was more a result of superior mobility, firepower and Iraqi ineptitude than of eliminating the fog of war. [144] Most importantly, it failed to account for the conditions on the battlefield after the fall of the regime.[145] Additionally, Ahmed Chalabi's perspective on the conditions in Iraq, Iraqi weapons of mass destruction, and his predictions about post-Saddam Iraq proved self serving and unrepresentative of actual conditions in Iraq.[146]

Alternative Analysis:

The most important aspect of alternative analysis is that it provides different ways of looking at a problem and potential solutions that decision makers might otherwise overlook. This enables them to explore options more fully before committing to a solution, and may even open their eyes to the "real" problem. Gordon and Trainor assert that the Bush Administration presided over a system in which differing military and political perspectives were discouraged. They say "perspective" but as it relates to this monograph, it is more about differing "analysis." They charge that the climate amongst the key figures in the Bush Administration squashed or marginalized differing analysis concerning planning for OIF. Squashing or marginalizing dissenting opinions simply because they are different without considering their merits is the converse of incorporating alternative analysis into decision-making.

---

[144] Gordon and Trainor, 352. The authors assert that U.S. forces could not adequately identify the location and strength of Fedayeen forces, and that U.S. forces even missed the movement of the Nebuchadnezzar Division from north of Baghdad to south of Baghdad. Further, they state that even when information was available, difficulties in transmitting the information to forward units in a timely manner proved troublesome. The result was that often times, lead units gained knowledge of enemy forces when they made contact, not before. This is hardly removing the "fog of war."

[145] Ibid., 500.

[146] Thomas Ricks, *Fiasco: The American Military Adventure in Iraq* (New York: Penguin Press, 2006), 56-57. Ricks states that Chalabi influenced the U.S. Government analysis of Iraqi WMD through the press and through direct access to parts of the U.S. Government. Further, he attributes Richard Perle as stating of Chalabi, "He is far and away the most effective individual that we could have hoped would emerge in Iraq…In my view, the person most likely to give us reliable advice is Ahmed Chalabi."

The first aspect of this charge is that the Bush Administration positioned key figures in the Department of Defense, namely General Meyers as the Chairman of the Joint Chiefs of Staff, precisely because they wanted to avoid dissenting opinions.[147] While it is arguable that selecting General Meyers as the JCS chairman was not solely for the purpose of squashing dissenting opinions, the net result was that little, if any, alternative analysis of OIF planning originated from the Joint Chiefs of Staff.

In addition to limiting alternative analysis, intentionally or not, by positioning key figures in the Department of Defense, the administration also disregarded differing analysis of key members inside the National Security Council. During pre-war planning, Colin Powell raised the issue of insufficient troop levels and potential post-war Iraq difficulties.[148] However, Secretary Rumsfeld, with the support of Vice President Cheney, countered Powell's analysis in favor of reliance on the mobility, speed, and technological advantage smaller forces provided. Colin Powell found himself outnumbered, resulting in inadequate consideration of his differing analysis of post war conditions.

The climate that caused marginalization of alternative analysis and divergent opinion was not limited to the National Security Council. CENTCOM suffered from similar problems. After the war began and the Fedayeen began to attack coalition forces with unconventional tactics, the CENTCOM Commander and the Coalition Forces Land Component Commander (CFLCC) had divergent views of the battlefield. To General Franks, the emergence of the Fedayeen did not

---

[147] Gordon and Trainor, 502. They state, "In the Iraq War, Rumsfeld and Franks dominated the planning; the Joint Chiefs of Staff were pushed to the margins and largely accepted their role. Richard Meyers was picked to be the JCS chairman because of his track record as a team player and largely fulfilled Rumsfeld's expectations."

[148] Ibid., 32 and 70-71. On page 32, Gordon and Trainor indicate that Colin Powel was concerned about the number of forces required early on in the planning, and that he warned General Franks to ensure that he had enough "muscle" that would be required. They state, "Powell's view of what was required was very different from Rumsfeld's." On pages 70-71, they indicate that Colin Powel was concerned about administering and rebuilding postwar Iraq and detail his conversation with President Bush about what he thought Iraq would look like after the regime toppled.

alter his conception that Baghdad was the enemy center of gravity. Gordon and Trainor quote General Franks as saying "The Fedayeen are little more than a speed bump on the way to Baghdad."[149] To the commanders on the ground in Iraq, however, the situation looked very different.

LTG Wallace, the V Corps Commander, stated to reporters, "The enemy we are fighting is a bit different than the one we war-gamed against, because of these paramilitary forces. We knew they were here, but we did not know how they would fight."[150] To LTG Wallace and LTG McKiernan, this seemed to be a statement of the obvious. To Donald Rumsfeld and General Franks, however, it was an attack against the U.S. strategy and a "repudiation of Frank's insistence that the war be 'fast and final.'"[151] General Franks subsequently informed LTG McKiernan that he was considering relieving LTG Wallace over the remarks.

LTG McKiernan quickly came to LTG Wallace's defense, where he also took the opportunity to explain the conditions on the battlefield and push for slowing down the attack to Baghdad in order to defeat the paramilitary forces. He informed General Franks that the enemy was fighting from the cities, and that there was not a Shiite uprising in the south as expected. Further, the regime still controlled its forces and Iraqi regular army forces had not surrendered or capitulated as expected. [152] General Franks replied that he did not believe the situation in the south was that serious and that the Fedayeen were not the problem. He believed that U.S. forces

---

[149] Gordon and Trainor, 305.

[150] Ibid, 311.

[151] Ibid, 312.

[152] Ibid, 313. After the emergence of the Fedeyeen, and the disruption to the original plan they caused, LTG McKiernan pushed General Franks to slow the attack to Baghdad in order to defeat the paramilitary forces in the south. The authors state, "McKiernan argued that the enemy was fighting an urban-centric battle, starting from the Euphrates. There had not been a Shiite uprising, and Saddam's ability to command his forces was still intact. Iraq's Regular Army divisions had neither surrendered nor capitulated."

were simply not aggressive enough. This sent the message loud and clear that alternative analysis from within the ranks was unwelcome.

Another indication that CENTCOM and the national command apparatus did not incorporate alternative analysis into decision-making is the failure to adapt to changing conditions on the battlefield. Gordon and Trainor assert that both CENTCOM and the Bush Administration "failed to adapt to developments on the ground and remained wedded to their prewar analysis even after Iraqis showed their penchant for guerrilla tactics in the first days of the war."[153] Several indicators surfaced early on in the war that should have tipped CENTCOM and the national command apparatus that the war was not going exactly to plan. Iraqis in the southern cities of Nasiriyah, Samawah and Najaf did not welcome U.S. forces as assumed. Instead, Iraqis dressed in civilian clothes used ambushes, improvised roadside bombs, and suicide attacks to put up stiff resistance.

While U.S. forces on the ground recognized differences between their expectations and the reality of what was happening and quickly adjusted their tactics, higher-level decision makers at CENTCOM and the national level did not adjust their war plan because they refused to accept alternative analysis of the situation on the ground.[154] General Frank's "speed bump on the way to Baghdad" comment is the most obvious indicator of his inability to accept analysis that differed from his conception, even in the face of obvious evidence that should have caused him to reconsider. This difference in the reality of what was happening on the ground as seen by the ground force commanders and the expectations of the enemy based on the CENTCOM planning caused divergent views of the battlefield that were never reconciled.

---

[153] Gordon and Trainor, 497-498.

[154] Ibid., 501. Gordon and Trainor assert that General Franks never acknowledged the enemy he faced or even comprehend the nature of the war.

One example of the impact of the divergent views of the battlefield between General

Franks and his subordinate commanders is the disagreement between CENTCOM and

subordinate commanders about employing the 4th Infantry Division after Turkey's refusal to

allow the division to enter Iraq through its territory. General Franks, still believing that the

Republican Guard was the primary enemy, wanted the 4th Infantry Division to remain afloat in the

Mediterranean Sea as a deception designed to hold Iraqi divisions north of Baghdad. [155] LTG

McKiernan and LTG Wallace, on the other hand, recognized the new threat, and wanted 4th

Infantry Division to follow V Corps north from Kuwait to combat the Fedayeen in the Corps rear

area. General Franks refused to budge, believing that there was no immediate need for the 4th

Infantry Division to fight the Fedayeen, and that it was simply V Corps lack of aggressiveness

that disrupted the CENTCOM plan. [156] General Franks decided to keep 4ID afloat, which

prevented V Corps from quickly securing their lines of communication and crushing the

beginnings of what would develop into a full-blown insurgency.

Further, once Baghdad fell and the regime collapsed, General Franks and senior officials

at the Department of Defense assumed the U.S. had achieved victory and focused their attention

on redeploying U.S. forces. [157] In fact, almost immediately after Baghdad fell, General Franks

issued instructions to his subordinate commanders to prepare to redeploy within 60 days and to

expect some form of functioning Iraqi government within that time. [158]

One manifestation of this redeployment focus was stopping the flow of the 1st Cavalry

Division as a follow on force. Senior members of the Department of Defense did not think

additional forces were required for postwar Iraq. In *Fiasco*, Thomas Ricks quotes Paul

---

[155] Gordon and Trainor, 306.

[156] Ibid., 313.

[157] Ibid., 501. The authors assert that as early as a week after U.S. forces captured Baghdad, the Department of Defense turned its focus to co-opting foreign forces to replace U.S. forces for the post conflict phase and redeploying U.S. forces.

[158] Ibid., 459.

Wolfowitz as saying, "I don't see why it would take more troops to occupy the country than to take down the regime."[159] Secretary Rumsfeld continued to maintain confidence in the original planning assumption that the Iraqi population would embrace U.S. forces as liberators and cooperate in setting up a democratic state, which provided the rationale for him to cancel follow on forces. During these deliberations, General Franks did not assert the requirement for additional forces…forces that his commanders on the ground desperately wanted. The senior planner for CFLCC, Colonel Kevin Benson, asserted that this failure to continue the flow of forces created the vacuum that enabled the budding insurgency to spring into a full-blown insurgency.[160]

Another of Gordon and Trainor's criticisms is that the U.S. did not bring the right "tools" to the fight and put too much confidence in technology. Secretary Rumsfeld's vision of transforming the U.S. Army revolved around speed, precision, and superior information to enable smaller forces to achieve decisive results. In his mind, Operation ENDURING FREEDOM largely vindicated his vision. A small number of U.S. special operations forces, supported by air power and intelligence, co-opted large numbers of indigenous forces and toppled the Taliban regime in Afghanistan very quickly. He believed that his theory would also apply to Iraq, despite objections from some members of Army leadership. Secretary Rumsfeld dismissed their objections as "legacy thinking."[161]

---

[159] Ricks, 121. Ricks asserts that Wolfowitz made this comment in a conversation about whether follow on forces should go to Iraq according to plan.

[160] Ibid., 122.

[161] Gordon and Trainor, 53. The JCS conducted a study named "Operational Availability" to evaluate the effects of smaller, faster forces aided by technology. The study confirmed Rumsfeld's vision that U.S. forces could win with substantially fewer forces if they struck fast, and repudiated the Powell doctrine that called for overwhelming force, which required a slow build up of forces. Many members of the Army's leadership in the JCS, however, believed that numbers and superior firepower still mattered and did not buy into the studies conclusions. Secretary Rumsfeld dismissed their challenge as "legacy thinking." Gordon and Trainor state, "Heartened by the small force stunning victory in Afghanistan, the rapid defeat of Iraq on his terms would break the spine of Army resistance to his transformation goal once

While the speed which U.S. forces defeated Iraqi regular forces and toppled the regime indicate that at least part of Secretary Rumsfeld's strategy was correct, it did not fully account for the conditions on the battlefield during the march to Baghdad and after the regime fell. First, the emergence of the Fedayeen posed an unforeseen challenge. They attacked unsecured lines of communication and support forces using guerilla and terrorist tactics. These unconventional methods largely neutralized the technological advantage of U.S. forces, as they were next to impossible to identify, locate, or monitor. Second, once the regime collapsed the advantage of speed over mass reversed itself. Mass was more critical to stabilizing postwar Iraq than speed.[162] Unfortunately, U.S. forces did not have forces available to make up for this troop shortfall because of the rush to get to Baghdad with fewer forces, which left critical areas of Iraq unsecured, created sanctuaries for the insurgency, and contributed to the general lawlessness and instability in large parts of Iraq.

In planning for OIF, CENTCOM and senior officials in the Department of Defense misapplied the red teaming core concept of incorporating alternative analysis into decision-making. Their error was that their "alternative" analysis of a new system of warfare simply did not fit the situation in Iraq. While the speed which CENTCOM toppled Saddam Hussein's regime indicate that speed, precision and technological superiority do enable smaller forces to win battles, it did not account for the conditions after those battles, which are as much a part of achieving victory as defeating enemy forces. Further, once the decision makers settled on their "alternative" analysis, they created an atmosphere that discouraged and marginalized challenges to it. These factors prevented CENTCOM and the Department of Defense from understanding the actual conditions on the battlefield and adjusting their analysis of the situation to better

---

and for all…As the result of technological advances in electronics and computerization, warfare was being elevated to a new level."

[162] Gordon and Trainor, 500.

account for shortfalls in their plan. As a result, the number of U.S. forces on the ground in Iraq proved insufficient to deal with the emerging Fedayeen threat during major combat operations, and to provide a secure environment after major combat operations ended. These two factors enabled the conditions for the budding insurgency to blossom into a full-blown insurgency.

Alternative Perspectives:

Alternative perspectives enable decision makers to develop a better understanding of the operational environment as seen through the lens of adversaries, partners, and other actors. This enhanced understanding improves decision making by enabling anticipation of second and third order effects. Yet anticipation of second and third order effects was conspicuously absent in planning for OIF. CENTCOM and the national command apparatus focused on one "Iraqi" perspective and failed to consider other legitimate alternative perspectives that may have clued them in on the long-range implications of their plan. Over-reliance on Ahmed Chalabi prevented them from seeking other perspectives that were more representative of the Iraqi population, which led to misunderstanding the enemy and underestimating the Iraqi population's propensity for resistance. Finally, the OIF plan unrealistically assumed that Iraqis and other nations, which were generally ambivalent about the invasion to start with, would bear much of the burden of reconstruction and stability, without considering their perspectives.

Just as alternative analysis must be accurate before it is useful, so must alternative perspectives accurately represent the viewpoint they purport to express before they are useful. Ahmed Chalabi provided one "Iraqi" perspective that the administration latched onto.[163] However, his perspective of the nature of the Iraqi regime, the Iraqi population's desire for

---

[163] David Phillips, *Losing Iraq: Inside the Postwar Reconstruction Fiasco* (New York: Westview Press, 2005), 67. Phillips states, "The Bush Administration never had a plan or program for running postwar Iraq; instead, it focused on a person – Ahmad Chalabi, who, it believed, could transform Iraq into a liberal democracy and support U.S. goals in the Middle East. U.S. officials did not trust unknown elements of the Iraqi polity, which they feared would be unfriendly to U.S. interests."

liberation from Saddam's tyranny, and the Iraqi WMD program all proved false and based on self-interest.[164] While it is easy to second-guess the decision to embrace Chalabi in hindsight, some departments of the U.S. government suspected that he was not representative of the Iraqi population and was acting in self-interest early on. Both the CIA and the State Department were suspicious of Chalabi because of his "slick" and "divisive" persona, and his implication in a bank fraud case in Jordan.[165] Further, they believed his forty-five year exile from Iraq put him out of touch with the true workings of the Saddam Hussein regime and the Iraqi population. However, the Defense Department brushed aside these reservations and accepted Chalabi as the "Iraqi" perspective. Much of the failure in incorporating alternative perspectives into planning and execution for OIF stems from this reliance on Ahmed Chalabi's perspective as a legitimate Iraqi perspective, because it falsely convinced the decision makers that they had a true understanding of Iraq through the eyes of an Iraqi.

One effect of over-reliance on Ahmed Chalabi to provide the Iraqi perspective was a failure to identify and prepare for all the elements of the enemy or understand the regime's complexity. Chalabi convinced senior officials in the Department of Defense that the Iraqi population desired liberation from Saddam's regime.[166] This caused decision makers to disregard the possibility of an insurgency and to focus on Iraq's conventional forces as the primary enemy. Similar to the 1991 Gulf War, CENTCOM viewed the Republican Guard as the "protector" of the regime and as their major adversary in OIF, largely disregarding other elements of Saddam's security apparatus. They expected to overwhelm Iraq's non-Republican Guard forces quickly, and then to fight the Republican Guard around Baghdad, after which the regime would collapse.

---

[164] Phillips, 68-72. On page 68, Phillips states that Chalabi convinced U.S. officials that the U.S. would be seen as "liberators" by the Iraqi population. Further, on page 72, Phillips states, "…Chalabi's self-interest was served by persuading the United States to invade Iraq."

[165] Bob Woodward, *Plan of Attack* (New York: Simon and Schuster, 2004), 20.

[166] Phillips, 72. Phillips states, "…Chalabi asserted that Iraqis were practically begging to be invaded; furthermore, after liberation, the country could be run on the cheap."

This view of the Republican Guard as the major adversary and protector of the regime was contrary to Saddam's view. Saddam viewed the Republican Guard as a tool to counter rebellious tribal groups within Iraq, as his primary weapon against external neighbors, but also as a potential threat to his power. For this reason, he placed stringent security restrictions on the Republican Guard and continuously spied on his commanders through an intricate network of regime security organizations. This stringent oversight and spying prevented commanders from controlling their own forces, coordinating with adjacent units, or putting up a coherent defense of Baghdad.[167]

In fact, Saddam viewed his primary threat as an internal coup, not the U.S. toppling his regime. He based this view on his perception of the U.S. lack of resolve in removing him from power in the 1991 Gulf War, and his perception of U.S. casualty aversion demonstrated in Somalia and Kosovo. He did not believe the U.S. had the political will to sustain the number of casualties he believed inevitable if the U.S. invaded, so he focused his planning on protecting his regime against other opportunistic external and internal threats.[168] The result of Saddam's threat analysis was his "ring" defense plan for Baghdad. The U.S. misinterpreted this "ring" plan for a "Mesopotamian Stalingrad" in which the inner most ring, designated as the "red line", was the trigger for releasing chemical or biological weapons to prevent U.S. forces from entering Baghdad.[169] However, based on debriefings from senior Iraqi regime officials, the "red line"

---

[167] Kevin Woods et al., *Iraqi Perspectives Project: A View of Operation Iraqi Freedom from Saddam's Senior Leadership* (U.S. Joing Forces Command: Joint Center for Operational Analysis, 2006), 27. The authors state, "Fear of a military coup so dominated Saddam's thinking that he imposed a series of security restrictions on Iraq's assorted military organizations, which severely hobbled preparations to defend the country…At a time when coalition military leaders were worried about Saddam using the Republican Guard to create a 'Mesopotamian Stalingrad,' he would not even allow his army to have maps of the city of Baghdad."

[168] Ibid., 29. The authors state "The fact that the United States had changed its policy on Somalia after sustaining what to him were incredibly minor losses amplified his contempt for American military might and the political will to use it."

[169] Gordon and Trainor, 136. Gordon and Trainor state, "U.S. intelligence analysts had grossly misinterpreted Saddam's new defensive strategy, assuming the ring plan that had so dismayed the Iraqi

simply delineated the line that Republican Guard forces could not retreat into Baghdad from.[170] Saddam actually prohibited Republican Guard forces entering Baghdad due to his fear of a military coup.

In reality, paramilitary forces represented the principal challenge in Southern Iraq during the major combat operations, and eventually evolved into the insurgency that still exists. CENTCOM believed that since the regime was an authoritarian, rigidly controlled, centralized power structure, seizing Baghdad and "decapitating" the regime would ensure victory. The CENTCOM plan maintained that Baghdad was the regime's "center of gravity" even after the regime collapsed.[171] While the analysis of the regime as centralized and authoritarian was largely true, the mechanism the regime employed to maintain power was not the military, but paramilitary organizations like the Fedayeen, which dispersed themselves and significant weapons caches throughout the cities to control the population.[172] Gordon and Trainor assert that the attacks by the Fedayeen during the march toward Baghdad showed the Fedayeen's fanatical dedication to the regime and their lack of dependence on the regime's rigid command and control structure.[173] In fact, once air strikes severed communications with the regime, the dispersion actually caused a less centralized command and control structure. The result was that the Fedayeen conducted a guerilla style campaign against coalition forces independent of regime control. While CENTCOM efforts to sever communications between conventional forces and the

generals in December was a scheme to unleash chemical and possibly biological weapons against U.S. troops as they closed in on the Iraqi capital."

[170] Gordon and Trainor, 124.

[171] Ibid., 499. The authors state, "Rumsfeld and Franks believed that their victory would be sealed with the seizure of Baghdad, which was identified as Iraq's 'center of gravity.' But from the first day of the invasion the United States was not fighting a purely conventional war, one that would be suddenly brought to an end when the regime's ministries were seized and its leader toppled."

[172] Ibid., 136. The authors assert that as the U.S. was busy worrying about the Republican Guard, it did not identify the efforts of the Fedayeen to distribute tons of arms caches in schools and mosques throughout the southern cities of Iraq. Further, the U.S. intelligence analysts dismissed the Fedayeen as playing only a minor role in Iraqi defense plan.

[173] Ibid., 499.

regime successfully paralyzed large parts of Iraq's conventional forces, it did not account for this second order effect because the OIF plan dismissed the importance of paramilitary forces.

Further, CENTCOM expected the population in southern Iraq to welcome U.S. forces as liberators, not occupiers. In fact, they expected some elements of the population in the south to assist coalition forces.[174] However, based on their perception that the U.S. "double-crossed" them during the first Gulf War, they were much more wary of U.S. intentions in OIF.[175] The result was that they did not welcome U.S. forces as expected, and U.S. forces ended up fighting costly battles with paramilitary forces in the southern cities of Nasariyah, Samawah, Najaf, Kifl, and Diwaniyah. Once the regime collapsed, much of the population initially warmed up to the U.S., happy to be free from Saddam's tyrannical regime. However, when the U.S. proved unable to re-establish order and civil services quickly, support for U.S. forces eroded.[176] This failure contributed to the development of the insurgency.

Finally, because of an over-reliance on Chalabi's perspective, the OIF plan failed to incorporate other, more relevant alternative perspectives into its design for post-war Iraq. Chalabi convinced senior officials in the Department of Defense that postwar reconstruction would require minimal support from the U.S. because the Iraqis could shoulder most of the

---

[174] Woodward, 62. Woodward lists the planning assumptions General Franks briefed President Bush on early on in the planning for OIF. Assumption number four states, "Some Iraqi opposition groups would support the U.S. military inside Iraq or at least would provide some cooperation."

[175] Ibid., 70. Woodward states, "After the 1991 Gulf War, President George H. Bush signed a presidential finding authorizing the CIA to topple Saddam…the president publicly called on Iraqis to 'take matters into their own hands' to remove Saddam. When the Kurds in the north and Shiite Muslims in the south rebelled against Saddam, Bush declined U.S. military support. The result was another slaughter."

[176] Gordon and Trainor, 506. The authors state, "As poorly positioned to keep order as the Americans were, many Iraqis at first were thankful for the removal of Saddam's regime or simply too numbed by the rapid turn of events and display of American power to complain. But when order and essential services were not immediately restored, American prestige eroded quickly…As local Iraqis were quick to note, the Americans could put a man on the moon but could not provide electricity."

burden themselves.[177] Thus, the CENTCOM plan sought to shift much of the burden of reconstruction and stability onto the Iraqi population and other nations.

Based on Chalabi's perspective, Secretary Rumsfeld and General Franks envisioned a functioning democratic form of government standing up in Iraq within three months of regime collapse, which would subsequently shoulder most of the reconstruction burden internally.[178] To make up for shortfalls, the plan relied on other nations to provide security forces, manpower, and funding.[179] Obviously, this was an overly optimistic assessment of the propensity for transitioning to democratic governance in Iraq. It failed to consider the impact of decades of repression and authoritarianism, and the largely ambivalent attitude towards the war held by many of the nations the U.S. planned to exploit for post-war reconstruction contributions.

The Ba'ath Party ruled Iraq with an iron fist for forty years. Decades of authoritarian rule and the severe sectarian repression used to keep various ethnic groups under control created an atmosphere of learned helplessness. Saddam viewed independence and resourcefulness as threats to his power and systematically beat out all traces of it from society. This created a lack of initiative and complete dependence on the state in just about every aspect of society. Even military commanders feared showing initiative or competence.[180] Yet the OIF postwar plan assumed that Iraqis would quickly step up and assume governance, financing, and security functions vacated by the collapsed regime. The failure to account for the perspective of the

---

[177] Phillips, 124.

[178] Gordon and Trainor, 503. Gordon and Trainer state, "The cost of reconstructing postwar Iraq was assessed at no more than $3 billion, which assumed that Iraq would soon be on its feet and able to pay its own way."

[179] Ibid., 503. The authors make the case that the unilateral foreign policy that the Bush Administration ascribed combined with their disdain for nation building actually required that the administration solicit the help of other nations in post war Iraq to fill the security and reconstruction voids.

[180] Woods, et al., 7. The authors argue that Saddam was wary of competent subordinates and instituted a policy of purges to control the perceived threat his military commanders might pose to him. They state, "[Saddam] undertook a policy first described by Herodotus 2,500 years ago of 'cutting the ears of grain that stuck out above the rest.'"

population living under such repressive rule for so long prevented the OIF plan from realistically appraising the capability of the Iraqi population to be self-sufficient, much less understand or adopt a democratic form of governance.

In addition to failing to consider the perspective of the Iraqi population in the post-war plan, the OIF plan also failed to consider adequately the perspective of the very nations the plan counted on for providing post-war security forces, manpower, and funding. As it became clear to the world that the U.S. was going to act preemptively in Iraq, few nations were in complete agreement that the U.S. had the necessity or the right to attack Iraq.[181] Yet the support of these nations was critical to the OIF postwar plan because of the limited forces Secretary Rumsfeld wanted to use in the invasion. Since these nations did not agree with the preemptive nature of the war, it was unrealistic to assume they would agree to provide postwar support. Further, these nations remained unwilling to commit resources or personnel for postwar reconstruction after the regime collapsed because security remained tenuous. The failure of the OIF planners to reconcile their assumption about the willingness of other nations to provide resources with an assessment of those nations perspective of the war resulted in the U.S. and Great Britain shouldering the bulk of postwar reconstruction and stabilization efforts without the necessary forces.

As stated earlier, incorporating alternative perspectives enables decision makers to develop a better understanding of the operational environment and anticipate long-term implications of their actions. However, decision makers must ensure that the alternative perspectives they consider accurately reflect the perspective they purport to represent. OIF decision makers relied too heavily on the perspective provided by Ahmed Chalabi, which prevented them from seeking other perspectives that were more representative of the Iraqi

---

[181] Gordon and Trainor, 504. The authors state, "…the consolidation of the United State's gains assumed that Washington would eventually elicit the cooperation of others: the Iraqis and allied nations that in the main were all too happy to keep their distance from postwar Iraq." Further, on page 93, they asset that Secretary Rumsfeld suggested early on in the planning to recruit Arab nations to do peacekeeping duty after the regime collapsed in order to "calm the 'Arab street.'"

population. This led to misunderstanding the enemy, underestimating the Iraqi population's propensity for resistance, and an unrealistic plan for Iraqis and other nations to bear the burden of reconstruction and stability for postwar Iraq.

Conclusion

One obvious discrepancy between the case studies presented in this monograph and the U.S. army's implementation of red teaming is the emphasis on *independent* red teams. In each of the case studies presented in this monograph, the "red team" was actually the commander applying the core concepts, seemingly without the aid of independent teams.[182] While independent red teams are beneficial because they expand the number of people thinking about the problem and mitigate the tendency to "group-think", they are not necessary if the commander is aware of and uses the basic concepts involved in red teaming. However, it is rare for a commander to be sufficiently dispassionate and introspective to enable "self red-teaming," which validates the need for an independent red team in most circumstances. Field Marshal Slim and T.E. Lawrence seemed to have this "self red-teaming" ability while General Franks did not. Regardless, the thinking behind the core concepts is the subject of this monograph, not the organization and employment of red teams.

The first two case studies presented in this monograph demonstrate that applying the core concepts of red teaming can significantly improve decision-making. However, the counterpoint, as the OIF case study demonstrates, is that there is danger in misapplying the core concepts. Basing their understanding on faulty analysis or perceptions from the start, decision makers can become over confident in their understanding of the operational environment, and subsequently refuse to consider other alternatives that more accurately account for the operational environment.

---

[182] Author's note: the sources for these case studies are works written by the commanders themselves, which may account for the absence of independent red teams mentioned in the texts. It is possible that Field Marshal Slim and T.E. Lawrence had colleagues and subordinates that provided this independent thought to their decision-making, but the authors did not mention them in their texts.

Realism and accuracy are critical to alternative analysis and alternative perspectives. The decision maker's ability to evaluate how realistic and accurate differing analysis and other perspectives are in assessing the operational environment can mean the difference between successful application of the red teaming core concepts and failure.

Field Marshal Slim's 1945 counteroffensive to destroy Japanese forces in Burma exemplifies how the core principles of red teaming can significantly improve decision-making. The dire circumstances under which Slim assumed command of the Fourteenth Army seemed to preclude any hope that a counteroffensive into Burma could succeed. However, Slim overcame the seemingly insurmountable odds by applying the core concepts of red teaming. Slim challenged the organization's thinking in the areas of the British capability to fight in the jungle and their over reliance on motor transportation and supplies. He incorporated alternative analysis to redefine his unit's use of air assets for movement, re-supply, and their casualty treatment. Finally, he incorporated Chinese and Japanese perspectives into his decision-making to develop a better understanding of the Japanese mindset, which he then effectively used against them by predicting Japanese strategies. Applying the core concepts of red teaming enabled Field Marshal Slim to turn the tables on the Japanese and destroy their forces in Burma.

Another example of successfully applying the core concepts of red teaming in decision-making is T.E. Lawrence's participation in the Arab Revolt of the World War I. Lawrence challenged the thinking in the British command in Egypt and the leaders of the Arab revolt by re-evaluating the capabilities and benefits of the Arab irregular forces. Additionally, he incorporated alternative analysis into his decision-making through re-evaluating the threat the Turks posed by occupying Medina, the strengths of the Arab irregulars and the Turkish forces, and the tactics the Arab irregulars used in attacking Turkish lines of communication. Remarkably, this analysis evolved into an alternative theory of irregular warfare. Finally, and most importantly, he incorporated the perspectives of the Arabs and the Turks into his analysis, which enabled him apply his new theory of irregular warfare to the Arab revolt. By applying the core concepts of red teaming, Lawrence reversed the seemingly inevitable failure of the Arab revolt and turned it into a major factor that forced the Turkish Army out of World War I.

The first two case studies in this monograph seem to indicate that applying the core concepts of red teaming enable commanders to develop a better understanding of the operational environment and improve decision-making. However, the OIF case study demonstrates that there is danger in applying these concepts. Secretary Rumsfeld's vision of military transformation is alternative analysis of the requirements for military power in future warfare. Results for Operation Enduring Freedom seemed to legitimize Secretary Rumsfeld's vision. However, while a relatively small number of U.S. forces quickly seized Baghdad and toppled Saddam Hussein's regime by operating according to Secretary Rumsfeld's theory, the conditions that evolved afterwards proved that his analysis did not account for the complex nature of Iraq. Additionally, the Defense Department's reliance on Ahmed Chalabi to provide the "Iraqi" perspective prevented the emergence of other perspectives that were more representative of the Iraqi population, which led to misunderstanding the enemy and underestimating the Iraqi population's propensity for resistance. These instances of misapplying the core concepts of red teaming indicate that decision makers must carefully evaluate the relevance and accuracy of alternative analysis and alternative perspectives because flawed analysis or skewed perspectives can cause decision makers to proceed down a path to failure.

While the OIF case study demonstrates the dangers of misapplying the core concepts of red teaming, it does not negate the fact that the red teaming core concepts can significantly improve understanding of the operational environment and lead to better decisions. Field Marshal Slim and T.E. Lawrence would likely have failed had they not challenged their organization's thinking, incorporated alternative analysis, and incorporated alternative perspective into their decision-making. Properly applied, these core concepts assist commanders in compensating for common pitfalls in their thinking, and enable better decisions. Therefore,

U.S. Army and Joint doctrine must incorporate these core concepts into their decision-making processes.

One place for red teaming in the current military decision making process is in wargaming. During wargaming, the commanders assess a friendly course of action against the adversary's potential responses, and its implications on the local population. Obviously, it is impossible to assess how the adversary might respond without considering the environment and the friendly course of action from the adversary's perspective. Thus, wargaming seems a natural place to incorporate the perspectives of the adversary, partners, the local population or other actors that influence the operational environment.

However, there is more to red teaming than this limited application during wargaming. The core concepts of red teaming enable decision makers to develop a better understanding of the operating environment before courses of action are developed. They assist decision makers in formulating their conception of the problem, understanding how the operational environment works, identifying vulnerabilities of adversaries and friendly forces, developing and exploring potential solutions, and anticipating potential long-term effects of actions. Therefore, commanders must apply the core concepts during each step of the military decision making process, not just during wargaming. In fact, the most critical times to apply the core concepts of red teaming are during receipt of mission and mission analysis because the decision maker develops his understanding of the operational environment during these two steps.

As the complexity of warfare continues to increase, it is more difficult to understand the operational environment and make good decisions in order to achieve success on the modern battlefield. Only through a complete understanding of the operating environment from the perspective of the U.S., its adversaries, and local inhabitants of the operational area combined with critical analysis in decision making and planning can the U.S. Army successfully accomplish the diverse and complex missions looming in the future. Applying the core concepts of red teaming can significantly improve a decision makers understanding of the operational environment and improve decision-making. Rooted in critical thinking, the core concepts of red teaming enable the decision maker to unshackle himself from common pitfalls to effective decision making such as methodism, ethnocentrism, cultural biases, and mirror imaging. Free from the "box" these pitfalls contain the decision maker in, he can now develop a better understanding of the operational environment through a more thorough exploration of alternative ideas for plans, operations, organizations and capabilities.

APPENDIX 1: Decision making theory and red teaming

As the U.S. Army definition of red teaming indicates, the purpose of a red team is ultimately to improve an organization's decisions. As such, the thinking behind red teaming draws its ideas from some of the more prominent decision making theorists. Dietrich Dörner's ideas in *The Logic of Failure: Why Things Go Wrong and What We Can Do to Make Them Right*, as well as Gary Klein's ideas in *Sources of Power: How People Make Decisions* contribute notably to the thinking behind red teaming.

In *The Logic of Failure: Why Things Go Wrong and What We Can Do to Make Them Right,* Dörner argues that as the complexity of world increased, human beings developed bad habits of thinking.[183] He asserts that these complex situations elicit bad thought habits which "set failure in motion from the beginning," and that the complexity of the task encourages decision-making methods that make failure inevitable.[184] These methods include acting without analyzing the situation adequately, failing to anticipate side effects and long term repercussions, assuming that the absence of immediately obvious negative effects means that correct measures were taken, letting over involvement with projects blind them to emerging needs and changes in the situation, and having cynical reactions to emerging information.[185] Red teaming seeks to correct these poor decision making methods.

In *Sources of Power: How People Make Decisions*, Klein argues that decision makers rely on a large set of abilities he calls "sources of power" to make decisions in natural settings, and that these sources of power are not analytic. They include using intuition, mental simulation, metaphor, and story telling.[186] Of these, mental simulation and metaphor have the most impact

---

[183] Dörner, 7.

[184] Ibid., 10.

[185] Ibid., 18.

[186] Klein, 3.

on the core concepts of red teaming. Klein defines mental simulation as "the ability to imagine people and objects consciously and to transform those people and objects through several transitions, finally picturing them in a different way than at the start."[187] The purpose of this effort is to observe what occurs as the sequence of transitions happens. It assists in imagining the effects that actions might have on the system and to generate explanations.[188]

One application of using mental simulation Klein describes as the "pre-mortem" strategy.[189] This strategy calls for mentally jumping into the future, imagining that the plan failed, and then explaining why.[190] The pre-mortem strategy has several benefits that enable better decision making. First, it mitigates the effects of "group think," defined by Dörner as "the tendency for a group of experts to reinforce one another's conviction that they are doing the right thing."[191] The pre-mortem strategy enables these experts to step outside of their personal commitment to the plan and see things that they may not have seen otherwise. This is a way of challenging the thinking of the organization. Second, by identifying weaknesses in the organization's reasoning and planning, the pre-mortem strategy encourages developing alternatives that they might not have developed otherwise. Thus, the benefits of Klein's pre-mortem strategy illustrate the basis for alternative analysis and challenging the organization's thinking, two of the core concepts of red teaming.

---

[187] Klein, 45.

[188] Ibid., 68.

[189] Ibid., 71.

[190] Ibid., 71.

[191] Dörner, 33-34.

APPENDIX 2: Background of Field Marshal Slim Case Study

On March 19, 1942, Field Marshal Viscount Slim assumed command of the British Army Burma Corps, later renamed Fifteenth Corps, which was engaged in a struggle to hold Burma against a better trained, better equipped, but numerically inferior Japanese force.[192] At the time, Slim knew almost nothing of the enemy he would fight for the next three years. He remarks in his personal account of the Burma campaign entitled *Defeat into Victory* prior to entering Burma for the first time, "I reflected…how very ignorant I was of the Japanese, their methods and their commanders."[193] He was about to learn much more about them. This case study examines how slim turned the devastating defeat the British suffered during the 1942 Burma campaign into their resounding victory in the 1945 campaign. Over the next three years, Field Marshal Slim would endure crippling defeats during a long and costly retreat from Burma into India, assume command of the Fourteenth Army, retrain his Army in India, and then counterattack to retake Burma in a brilliant campaign that turned "defeat into victory" for the British Army in Burma.[194] Field Marshal Slim's 1945 counteroffensive demonstrates the value of challenging the organizations thinking and using alternative perspectives to assist in decision-making.

Between the initial Japanese attack into Burma on January 20 of 1942, and Field Marshal Slim's arrival, the Japanese were soundly beating back the Burma Army, handing them defeat after defeat in every battle. At that time, the Burma Army consisted of two British and four Indian battalions, eight Burma Rifle battalions, and three Indian Mountain artillery batteries, later reinforced by the 16th Indian Brigade, the 17th Indian Division and the 7th Armored Brigade.[195] The Fifteenth Army, consisting of the 33rd Division and the 55th Division, led the Japanese

---

[192] Calvert, 31.

[193] Slim, 20.

[194] Ibid., 551.

[195] Calvert, 25.

forces. The total Japanese force consisting of 35,440 men attacked into the numerically superior 120,000 men of the British Burma Army, of which many were support troops or untrained in warfare.[196] To make up for numerical inferiority, the Japanese Fifth Air Division maintained air superiority over Burma during this period, as the Royal Air Force was engaged in the Indian Ocean.[197]

Slim's arrival in Burma did nothing to slow the Japanese advance, and the Japanese pushed the Burma Army entirely out of Burma. By the time he arrived, the stage was already set for the Burma Army's defeat, and Slim led the defeated army on a long and dangerous retreat out of Burma with the Japanese Fifteenth Army nipping at their heels and the torrential monsoons confounding every move. As noted by Ronald Lewin in *Slim the Standardbearer,* "Once the Japanese decided to move aggressively into Burma no commander, living or dead, could have sustained by his genius the indefensible British position. It was a house of cards, erected on the quicksands of false hope."[198]

The retreat to India was a devastating and costly blow to Slim's Burma Corps. The three and a half month, nine hundred mile withdrawal resulted in an estimated 13,000 killed, wounded and missing. Japanese pursuit, torrential monsoons, and a pathetic supply chain contributed to these casualties. The remnants of Slim's two divisions that made it out of Burma were in pathetic shape, plagued by malaria, dysentery and exhaustion. Slim estimated that about eighty percent of the survivors fell sick upon arrival in Imphal, and many of those died.[199] Further, the Corps' equipment was in an equally bad state. Japanese pressure forced them to abandon what tanks remained. Only twenty-eight out of the Corps' one hundred fifty field guns made it to India. In

---

[196] Calvert, 25.

[197] Ibid., 25.

[198] Lewin, 79.

[199] Slim, 113.

addition, the Corps' remaining mechanical transportation fleet consisted of only fifty trucks and thirty jeeps. [200]

Although Slim was not responsible for the errors that put the Burma Corps in such precarious circumstances, he accepted his share of responsibility for its defeat. He states, "The outstanding and incontrovertible fact was that we had taken a thorough beating. We, the Allies, had been outmaneuvered, outfought, and outgeneraled."[201] While the Japanese were better prepared, had better strategy and tactics, and executed them better, Slim learned many lessons during the Burma Corps' retreat. He was determined to use the lessons of those defeats and turn them to his advantage later on. Slim notes, "…remember only the lessons to be learnt from defeat – they are more than from victory."[202] Later, after Slim became the Fourteenth Army commander responsible for the upcoming Burma counter-offensive, he did just that.

In addition to building and training his new Fourteenth Army to fight the "the most formidable fighting insect in history" as Slim liked to call the Japanese, he had to prepare his troops for the environmental conditions facing them in Burma. Slim describes Burma as "…the worlds worst country, breeding the world's worst diseases, and having for half the year at least the world's worst climate."[203] Burma offered some of the worst fighting conditions Slim had ever experienced, and he knew that these conditions could be decisive if his men failed to prepare properly for them.

After the long retreat and demoralizing defeat, Slim had time to reflect on the causes contributing to the Burma Corps debacle. This reflection enabled him to develop his plans for retraining his Fifteenth Corps and subsequently the Fourteenth Army and to devise an operational

---

[200] Slim, 113-114.

[201] Ibid., 115.

[202] Ibid., 121.

[203] Ibid., 169.

design that would enable destruction of the Japanese forces in Burma. He identified the major causes of the Burma Corps defeat as a lack of preparation, smallness and unsuitability of the forces provided to defend Burma, lack of support from the local population, better Japanese generalship, inability to counter Japanese "hook" and "roadblock" tactics, and a lack of national purpose.[204]

The first cause for the 1942 campaign defeat Slim identified as a lack of preparation before the Japanese invaded. For starters, no one expected the Japanese to invade Burma.[205] While military forces in Burma fell under the administrative control of British forces in India, various headquarters passed responsibility back and forth, which resulted in a lack of focus by any headquarters to plan for the defense of Burma. This resulted in the military separation of Burma from India and the separation of operational from administrative control of forces in Burma.[206] In addition, the British command in India did not attempt to connect India to Burma by road. The Burma Army defended at the Southern end of Burma around Rangoon, some nine hundred miles from India, and because there was no road connecting Burma and India when Rangoon fell, the Burma Army was isolated.[207] This caused an inability to supply adequately the cut off army, hamstrung any attempt to regain their footing, and exacerbated the miserable conditions they endured on the long retreat.

This lack of preparation contributed to a second cause for the 1942 campaign defeat, which was the "smallness and unsuitability of the forces provided to defend Burma."[208] Slim

---

[204] Slim, 115-121.

[205] Ibid., 115. Slim states that until a few weeks before the invasion, no "higher authority, civil or military" expected the Japanese to invade Burma.

[206] Ibid., 115. Slim states that two effects resulting from the various commands pushing responsibility back and forth was the separation of Burma from India and the division of operational from administrative control. The British command in India retained administrative control of all forces in Burma, but took no responsibility for the defense of Burma (operational control).

[207] Ibid., 115.

[208] Ibid., 115.

describes the Burma Army as, "Two ill-found, hurriedly collected, and inexperienced divisions, of which one had been trained and equipped for desert warfare and the other contained a large proportion of raw and unreliable Burmese troops."[209] First, the Burmese forces were not equipped or trained for full-scale war, as they were raw recruits with no military experience and were hastily absorbed into the existing civil armed corps consisting of the Burma Military Police and the Burma Frontier Force.[210] The reliable forces were almost as ill prepared as the Burmese forces as they did not possess the skills for the environment they faced in Burma. They had no experience fighting in the jungle, so they considered it "impenetrable," whereas the Japanese viewed the jungle as "a welcome means of concealed maneuver and surprise."[211] In addition, these forces relied extensively on motor transportation and large supply trains, which were not well suited to the jungle environment. These ground forces were entirely inadequate to put up much of a fight against the Japanese.

Given the inadequacy of the Burma Army and its lack of preparation to defend Burma from the Japanese attack, the air forces could have assisted greatly. However, the air forces of Burma did not contribute much to compensate for the ground forces' inferiority. Initially, the Royal Air Forces assigned to Burma, meager as they were, did provide some air support. They were successful in conducting limited close air support and air attacks against Japanese airfields early on. Unfortunately, however, a retaliatory Japanese air attack caught them on the ground and destroyed the Royal Air Forces in Burma almost in its entirety.[212] This resulted is a complete lack of British air capability in Burma, and air superiority for the Japanese. During the

---

[209] Slim, 115-116.

[210] Ibid., 117.

[211] Ibid., 118.

[212] Ibid., 41.

subsequent retreat, Japanese air forces continuously pounded British forces, and the British could do nothing about it.

Another cause Slim identified as contributing to the 1942 defeat was that the population did not actively support the British. Slim states, "the inhabitants should have been not only on our side, but organized and trained to help us."[213] While only a small minority was actively hostile to the British, the vast majority tried to avoid involvement and contact with either side. The causes of this neutrality stem from the suddenness and inexplicability of the Japanese invasion from the perspective of the population, the inability of the British to defend Burma, and the immediate collapse of the civil government.[214] As the Japanese invasion beat back the British forces, the Burmese population, including the families of the Burmese civil armed corps, was left in "the dangerous no-man's land between the lines or in the crudely and brutally administered Japanese-occupied territory."[215] In essence, the population and civil government were completely unprepared for the invasion, which prevented any coherent support from the population that the British needed.

Another cause contributing to the defeat Slim identified as a difference in Japanese and British generalship. He describes the Japanese generals as "confident, bold to the point of foolhardiness, as so aggressive that never for one day did they lose the initiative."[216] Additionally, the Japanese had a clear and definite objective in mind, the destruction of British forces, and they pursued that objective relentlessly. In contrast, a lack of a clear purpose hampered the British generals. Slim describes their purpose as "a rather nebulous idea of retaining territory."[217] This led to the initial dispersion of the British forces, allowing the

---

[213] Slim, 116.

[214] Ibid., 116-117.

[215] Ibid., 117.

[216] Ibid., 118.

[217] Ibid., 118.

Japanese to mass on smaller formations, and a generally defensive mindset, which prevented the British from ever gaining the initiative.[218]

In addition to the operational level dominance by Japanese generals, tactically the Japanese also bested the British forces. The primary Japanese tactic consisted of what Slim describes as the "hook" and "road block."[219] The "hook" entailed establishing frontal contact in order to fix the British forces, then sending a mobile infantry force on a wide turning movement around the flank through the jungle to attack the British line of communication. After getting in behind the fixed force, the Japanese would establish a "road-block" on the single line of communication that supplied the British force with ammunition and reinforcements. The British forces had no choice but to turn and try to clear the roadblock, and when they did, the Japanese increased pressure on the front until it collapsed. Slim realized that the British forces had no defense for these tactics because of an over reliance on motor transportation and inability to fight and move in the jungle.[220] In addition, a complete lack of intelligence on Japanese movements prevented the British from identifying when and where the "hook" forces would emerge. The inability of the British to counter the Japanese "hook" and "roadblock" tactics prevented them from seizing the initiative.

Finally, Slim identified the lack of a national direction or purpose after the initial surprise of the invasion and loss of Rangoon as a contributing factor to the 1942 campaign defeat.[221] General Alexander, replacing Lieutenant General Hutton as Commander of the Burma Army, arrived in Burma with the task to hold Rangoon, as it was widely believed that the loss of Rangoon would cause all of Burma to fall. Unfortunately, by the time he arrived, the decisive

---

[218] Slim, 118.

[219] Ibid., 119.

[220] Ibid., 119.

[221] Ibid., 118-119.

battle of the Sittang Bridge was already lost and the fate of Rangoon sealed. [222] However, he received no updated clearly stated purpose for the Burma Army. Options included trying to destroy the Japanese army and recover lost territory, to establish a defensive line further north and retain at least part of Burma, or conduct a slow withdrawal to enable forces in India to prepare for its defense. [223] He was left to discern for himself what his purpose should be, and the result was that the local commanders could not define their purpose with sufficient clarity to present a coherent strategy against the Japanese.

Armed with the knowledge of how these causes contributed to the 1942 campaign defeat, especially the tactical lessons, Slim turned his energy towards preventing similar mistakes on the imminent counterattack. The first task Slim undertook in his massive retraining program was turning his inefficient and immobile corps headquarters into a fighting headquarters. [224] This included weapons and physical training for everybody as Slim understood from the retreat that there was no such thing as a "non-combatant" in Burma. [225] Next, he ensured that the headquarters was mobile by eliminating dependence on motor transportation and ensuring that all equipment was packed into "yakdans" which were saddlebags that could be carried by pack animals. [226] This ensured that the Corps Headquarters could quickly load any type of available transportation and it eliminated excess equipment that slowed the Corps down.

Next, Slim tackled the efficiency problem. He implemented technical training of the staff in their individual jobs, and even put the wives of soldiers lucky enough to have them in India to work in hospitals, canteens, or as clerks. [227] Additionally, he developed the "nerve center"

---

[222] Slim., 118.

[223] Ibid., 118.

[224] Ibid., 138.

[225] Ibid., 139.

[226] Ibid., 140.

[227] Ibid., 140.

concept consisting of the war room and the information room.[228] The war room was the true

operations center for the corps, and was restricted to the corps staff sections. It tracked the battle

and facilitated Slim's decision-making. The information room, on the other hand, was open to

everyone, and it provided enough information to keep anyone with an interest informed of the

situation. Slim believed that keeping everyone "in the know" facilitated increased

performance.[229] Within three months, Slim's corps headquarters was mobile and efficient.[230]

The next task was to train his subordinate organizations to fight in the jungle, and Slim

based this training on the tactical lessons from the 1942 campaign. The first lesson was that the

jungle was neither impenetrable nor unfriendly, and the individual soldier must learn to live,

move, and fight in it.[231] He maximized field training in jungle conditions until it became second

nature to his troops. Second, Slim believed that "patrolling was the master key to jungle

fighting," and he emphasized small unit jungle operations.[232] Third, Slim understood that the

Japanese "hook" and "road-block" tactics were disconcerting to his forces, so he emphasized that

his units must get used to having Japanese forces behind them, and "regard not themselves, but

the Japanese, as surrounded."[233] Fourth, he realized that lines of communication would always

be vulnerable, and he did not have sufficient troops available to protect their entirety. He

emphasized dealing with penetrations with mobile local reserves.[234] Fifth, he learned that frontal

attacks, especially on narrow fronts, would not work, so he emphasized conducting his own

---

[228] Slim, 141.

[229] Ibid., 141.

[230] Ibid., 141.

[231] Ibid., 142.

[232] Ibid., 142.

[233] Ibid., 142.

[234] Ibid., 142.

"hook" attacks similar to the Japanese tactic.[235] Sixth, he learned that tanks were a valuable asset, but they had to be concentrated and supported by infantry.[236] His training focused on infantry and armor cooperation. Seventh, as stated earlier, Slim learned that there were no non-combatants in jungle warfare, so he emphasized that all units and sub-units had to provide their own protection and conduct their own patrolling.[237] Finally, he recognized that his forces must wrest the initiative from the Japanese in all circumstances. He states, when the Japanese have the initiative, "they are formidable. When we have it, they are confused and easily killed."[238] Based on these tactical lessons, Slim implemented a training program that was continuous and progressive, consisting of infantry battle schools, artillery training, air support training, combined arms training, river crossing training, and others.[239] His units lived for weeks on end in the jungle to learn how to operate in it. By the end of it, his corps was conducting inter-divisional exercises over large areas and under tough environmental conditions.

Before the counterattack into Burma occurred, Slim took over as Commander of the newly formed fourteenth Army after a failed attempt by the previous commander, Lieutenant General Irwin, to seize Akyab Island using the same tactics that failed so miserably in the 1942 campaign.[240] Lieutenant General Irwin was relieved, and Slim took over his job. While Slim was disappointed in leaving the corps he took pride in forming into a well-prepared fighting machine, he now had the opportunity to impart his insights on a larger audience.[241] He would be

---

[235] Slim, 142.

[236] Ibid., 142.

[237] Ibid., 143.

[238] Ibid., 143.

[239] Ibid., 146.

[240] Calvert, 48-52.

[241] Slim, 167. Slim states, "I left with many regrets, not only at parting from my staff...but at not having had the chance of wielding with my own hand the weapon I had seen forged."

in a position to ensure that all forces involved in the counterattack were prepared in a similar fashion.

Armed with this new understanding of the environment, his adversary, and his own unit's capabilities, Slim counterattacked into Burma with the purpose of not just retaking Burma from the Japanese, but destroying the Japanese Army in Burma.[242] The campaign would take eight months, consist of several key battles on which the fate of the campaign would rest, and cost the Fourteenth Army many casualties. It would cost the Japanese much more, however. Slim's Fourteenth Army mostly destroyed the Japanese forces in Burma, and by the end of March 1945, the Japanese commander General Kimura accepted defeat.[243] The remainder of the Burma campaign consisted of mopping up stragglers, destroying the final Japanese attempt to break out of Burma, and preparing for an invasion of Malaya.

---

[242] Slim, 184.
[243] Ibid., 486.

APPENDIX 3: Background of T.E. Lawrence Case Study

The Arab Revolt against the Turks in World War I began in June of 1916. The evolution of the revolt lay in British desires to knock Turkey out of the war, which would enable them to focus their efforts on Germany. In *Seven Pilars of Wisdom*, T.E. Lawrence states, "Some Englishmen…believed that a rebellion of Arabs against Turks would enable England, while fighting Germany, simultaneously to defeat her ally Turkey."[244] Amid British assurances of help, Arab tribesman, considered poorly armed and inexperienced in warfare, conducted a surprise attack on the Turkish garrisons in Medina and Mecca.[245] Not surprisingly, their attack failed miserably, and the Arab forces then conducted a blockade of the Medina and Mecca garrisons. While their blockade successfully forced the Turkish garrison at Mecca to surrender, the Medina garrison, linked by lines of communication to the main Turkish forces in Syria, received reinforcements and held out.[246] Eventually, the Turks transitioned to offensive operations forcing the Arab forces to withdraw into the hills about fifty miles south-west along the road to Mecca, where the Arab revolt stagnated and the Turks prepared to "crush the revolt where it had started" in Mecca.[247]

At this point in the campaign, the general plan for the Arab forces, under advisement of British forces in Egypt, was to conduct a delay with Feisal's tribesman from these hills in order to slow the Turkish advance on Mecca and allow time for Sherif Ali, Feisal's eldest brother, to build an Arab regular army in Rabegh. Ragegh is a port city on the Red Sea, which controls the road from Medina to Mecca, which the British military advisors viewed as critical to the defense of Mecca. Lawrence states, "…no hostile force could pass along the main road without occupying it

---

[244] Lawrence, 1926. 26.

[245] Lawrence, 1920. 1.

[246] Ibid., 1.

[247] Ibid., 1.

and watering at its wells under the palm trees. Its defence (sic) was therefore of the main importance."[248] The British advisors believed that Arab tribesman would never be able to defeat Turkish forces by defending the hills, which necessitated developing an Arab regular force to defend Rabegh. Unfortunately, time was short for building and training this Arab regular force as the Turks had already begun preparation for their offensive down the Medina-Mecca road. If the Turks attacked before the Arab regular force was ready, Rabegh's defense would then require a British or Allied brigade, which the British were hesitant to provide.[249]

Under these circumstances, T.E. Lawrence entered the picture. He went to Arabia from Egypt to determine if Sharif Ali could build the Arab Regular Army and if Feisal's men could hold in the hills long enough to enable Sharif Ali to do so. In Lawrence's view, he believed that Feisal's position was very strong and could hold the Turks indefinitely with minimal British support, consisting of light machine guns and regular officers as advisors, while Sharif Ali created the Arab Regular Army. He states, "They were posted in hills and defiles of such natural strength that it seemed to me very improbable that the Turks could force them out, just by their superior numbers."[250] Based on Lawrence's report, the British command in Egypt continued with the plan of building the Arab Regular Army, counting on Feisal's men to delay any Turkish advance down the Medina-Mecca road long enough to build and train a sufficient force of Arab regulars to defend Rabegh.

While the training of the Arab regular force progressed, but was not sufficiently complete enough to enable a coherent defense of Rabegh, the Turks attacked down the Medina-Mecca road, intent on retaking Mecca, with an entire corps. Lawrence's theory on the capability of the Arab tribesman to defend terrain was quickly tested. Lawrence believed Feisal's force could hold

---

[248] Lawrence 1920, 2.

[249] Ibid., 2.

[250] Ibid., 3.

the hills and tie up the Turks indefinitely. The Turks actually broke through in only one day and continued their advance toward Rabegh unchecked.[251] This put the Arab revolt in precarious circumstances because the Arab Regular Army was not yet capable of defending Rabegh, no British force could arrive in time to defend it, the Turks would quickly move through Rabegh towards Mecca, and any introduction of British ground forces into the Hejaz would have caused the Arab revolt to fall apart.[252]

Given these dire circumstances, Lawrence decided that the only hope left was to try to threaten the Turkish flanks and thereby force the Turks into a defensive posture to deal with the threat. He states, "In the emergency it occurred to me that perhaps the virtue of irregulars lay in depth, not in face, and that it had been the threat of attack by them upon the Turkish northern flank which had made the enemy hesitate for so long."[253] Lawrence felt that the Arab tribesman could capitalize on this threat by moving toward the Hejaz railway North of Medina, thereby forcing the Turks into a defensive posture to defend their railway and allowing the Arab forces to regain the initiative.[254] He states, "…we decided that to regain the initiative we must ignore the main body of the enemy, and concentrate far off on his railway flank. The first step towards this was to move our base to Wejh."[255] Thus, Lawrence persuaded Feisal to take all of his tribesmen north two hundred miles to the town of Wejh, which threatened the Hejaz railway north of

---

[251] Lawrence 1920, 3.

[252] Ibid., 3. Lawrence states, "The Rabegh force was not capable of repelling the attack of a single battalion, much less of a corps. It was nearly impossible to send down British troops from Egypt at the moment: nor do I think that a single British brigade would have been capable of holding all the Rabegh position: nor was the Rabegh position indespesable to the Turks: nor would a single Arab have remained with the Sherif if he introduced British troops into the Hejaz."

[253] Ibid., 4.

[254] Ibid., 4. Lawrence states, "…if we moved towards the Hejaz railway behind Medina, we might stretch our threat (and accordingly, their flank) as far, potentially, as Damascus, eight hundred miles away to the North."

[255] Lawrence 1926, 116.

Medina. From there, the tribesmen would try to harass the Turkish lines of communication by disrupting the Hejaz railway.

The Turks responded by moving their forces back to Medina, and further splitting their force to protect Medina and guard the railway simultaneously. Lawrence states, "One half took up the entrenched positions about the city, which they held until after the Armistice. The other half was distributed along the railway to defend it against our threat."[256] Unbeknown to Lawrence and Feisal at the time, this move to Wejh proved to be the turning point for the Arab revolt. For the duration of the war, Feisal's tribesmen continually harassed the Hejaz railway and captured cut off Turkish garrisons. He states, "For the rest of the war the Turks stood on the defensive against us, and we won advantage over advantage till, when peace came, we had taken thirty-five thousand prisoners, killed and wounded and worn out about as many, and occupied a hundred thousand square miles of the enemy's territory, at little loss to ourselves." [257]

---

[256] Lawrence 1920, 4.

[257] Ibid., 4.

BIBLIOGRAPHY

Burtsell, R.L. *The Catholic Encyclopedia Volume I.* Translated by the Cloistered Dominican Nuns of the Monastery of the Infant Jesus, Lufkin, Texas. New York: Robert Appleton Company, 1907.

Calvert, Michael. *Slim.* New York: Ballantine Books, 1973.

Dörner, Dietrich. *The Logic of Failure: Why Things Go Wrong and What We Can Do To Make Them Right.* New York: Metropolitan Books, 1996.

Elder, Linda and Richard Paul. *The Miniature Guide to Critical Thinking Concepts and Tools.* Dillon Beach, California: The Foundation for Critical Thinking, 2005.

Fontenot, Gregory. "Seeing Red: Creating a Red-Team Capability for the Blue Force." *Military Review* 85, no. 5 (2005): 4-8.

Gold, Ted and Bob Hermann. *Defense Science Board Task Force on the Role and Status of DoD Red Teaming Activities.* Washington D.C.: Office of the Under Secretary of Defense for Acquisition Technology and Logistics, 2003.

Gordon, Michael R. and Bernard E. Trainor. *Cobra II: The Inside story of the Invasion and Occupation of Iraq.* New York: Pantheon Books, Random House, 2006.

Holland, John H. *Hidden Order: How Adaptation Builds Complexity.* Reading, Massachusetts: Addison-Wesley Publishing Co., 1995.

Klein, Gary. *Sources of Power: How People Make Decisions.* Cambridge, Massachusetts: The MIT Press, 1999.

Lawrence, T.E. "The Evolution of a Revolt." *Army Quarterly and Defence Journal* (October 1920): Combat Studies Institute Reprint.

Lawrence, T.E. *Seven Pillars of Wisdom.* Harmondsworth, Middlesex, England: Penguin Books, Ltd., 1926.

Lewin, Ronald. *Slim: The Standardbearer.* London: Leo Cooper, Ltd., Octopus Publishing Group, 1976.

Lewis, Michael. *Moneyball: The Art of Winning an Unfair Game.* New York: W.W. Norton and Company, 2003.

Phillips, David L. *Losing Iraq: Inside the Postwar Reconstruction Fiasco.* New York: Westview Press, 2005.

Ricks, Thomas E. *Fiasco: The American Military Adventure in Iraq.* New York: Penguin Press. 2006.

Sandoz, John F. *Red Teaming: Shaping the Transformation Process.* Alexandria Virginia: Institute for Defense Analysis, Advanced Warfighting Program, 2001.

Sorrells, William T. et al. "Systemic Operational Design: An Introduction." School of Advanced Military Studies Monograph, U.S. Army Command and General Staff College, 2005.

Slim, William J. S. *Defeat into victory: Battling Japan in Burma and India, 1942-1945.* 1956. Reprint, New York: Cooper Square Press: Distributed by National Book Network, 2000.

Tsu, Sun. *The Art of War.* Edited by Ralph D. Sawyer. New York: Westview Press, 1994.

University of Foreign Military and Cultural Studies. *Red Team Handbook: version 3 draft*. Fort Leavenworth, Kansas: U.S. Army Training and Doctrine Command, 2007.

U.S. Department of the Army. *FM 5-0 Army Planning and Orders Production*. Washington D.C.: Government Printing Office, January 2005.

U.S. Department of the Navy. Headquarters, United States Marine Corps. *MCWP 5-1, Marine Corps Planning Process*. Washington D.C.: Government Printing Office, 24 September 2001

U.S. National Security Council. *"National Strategy for Victory in Iraq-November 2005."* http://www.whitehouse.gov/infocus/iraq/iraq_strategy_nov2005.html (Accessed February 8, 2008)

Von Clausewitz, Carl. *On War*. Edited by Michael Howard and Peter Paret. Princeton, New Jersey: Princeton University Press, 1976.

Woods, Kevin M. et al. *Iraqi Perspectives Project: A View of Operation Iraqi Freedom from Saddam's Senior Leadership*. U.S. Joint Forces Command: Joint Center for Operational Analysis, 2006.

Woodward, Bob. *Plan of Attack*. New York: Simon and Schuster, 2004.